STOP, GO, TURN

STOP, GO, TURN

Perfecting the Basics of Riding

CLAIRE LILLEY

J.A. ALLEN LONDON

First published in 2014 by
J.A. Allen
Clerkenwell House
Clerkenwell Green
London EC1R 0HT
www.allenbooks.co.uk

J.A. Allen is an imprint of Robert Hale Limited

ISBN 978-1-908809-13-1

A catalogue record for this book is available from the British Library

Edited by Jane Lake
Designed and typeset by Paul Saunders
Photographs by Dougald Ballardie
Diagrams by Carole Vincer

Printed in China by 1010 Printing International Ltd

Acknowledgements

I would like to thank Lesley Gowers of J. A. Allen who encouraged me to write this book, Jane Lake for doing a great editing job on my random thought processes and Carole Vincer for the easy-to-understand diagrams. I owe a debt of gratitude to my friend and colleague, Lorraine Mahoney, who demonstrated all the rider exercises with me, and last but not least, to my husband, Dougald Ballardie, and his trusty camera for taking such great photos. My horses, Heinrich and Norman also deserve a mention for being so obliging during the photo shoots.

Claire Lilley has produced a DVD to accompany this book. The fifth in her series of Training Programme DVDs, *Stop, Go, Turn* is available from **www.classicalseat.co.uk**

For more information about Claire Lilley, go to **www.clairelilley.com**

Contents

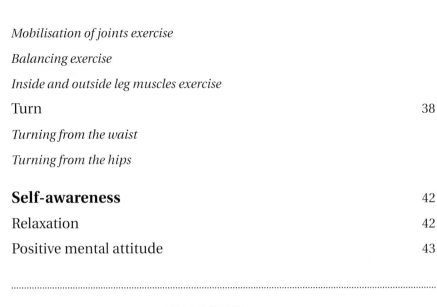

SECTION ONE **STOP**   47

The Importance of Stop, Go and Turn

Introduction

You may have picked up this book because you are experiencing problems with your riding to which you have not yet found a solution but, having flicked through it, you might think the information is very elementary. However, the best way to remedy most issues is to go back to basics. Never be afraid to go back a step in your horse's, or your own, training. Whatever level you ride at, and whichever discipline you enjoy, it is so important to make sure your basic riding technique is correct in order to get the very best from a horse.

Improving that basic riding technique is all about perfecting it over time. There is no quick fix; it takes months or even years to develop. You have to learn to work as a team with every horse you ride, whether you are a novice rider just starting out, or an advanced rider wanting to improve.

This book will give you a greater insight as to how three aspects of riding, stopping, moving and turning, are used both separately and interlinked to enable you to establish a correct training regime, whether you are starting a young horse, or retraining an older individual.

The outcome of being able to stop, go and turn with ease is a horse that is well balanced, attentive to the rider's aids and able to work through his back, i.e. the energy from the horse's quarters and hind limbs travels without restriction through the horse's back. This can only be achieved under a rider with a correct position and clear aids; clear aids create a confident and happy horse – and a happy rider!

Each section includes a listing of common problems plus ridden exercises to try.

Why do we Need to Stop, Go and Turn?

Stop aids

Stop aids are fundamental for safety; if you cannot stop your horse with ease, accidents will surely happen! Being able to halt squarely and in a correct outline is essential to develop your horse's muscles in the right way in the same way as standing in good posture yourself improves your own body tone and balance (Photo I.1).

Stop aids are also important when slowing down and speeding up. They are applied to slow down or stop, and released to speed up or go forwards. When a stop aid is used in this way, i.e. to control the horse, it is called a half-halt. The aids for a half-halt are the same as they are for a halt, but released before the horse actually comes to a standstill.

Half-halts are essential for improving your horse's balance and are necessary to prepare your horse for every transition and movement. They also regulate the gaits, and improve your horse's balance by encouraging him to take weight behind, i.e. transferring the weight back to the hind end to lighten the forehand.

Stop aids are used in conjunction with go aids to create transitions from one gait to another, or within each gait.

I.1 Stop aids: a good halt.

Go aids

Go aids are essential to ride your horse forwards in any gait, and also combine with stop aids to create transitions from one gait to another, or to slow down or speed up (Photo I.2).

After every halt and half-halt, your horse will need to go forwards again.

Your horse must always go forwards in rhythm. Each gait must remain pure at all times when you ride school movements, whether they are simple ones such as straight lines, turns and circles, or more demanding ones such as lateral movements.

In transitions your horse should go from one gait to the next seamlessly. If the horse is going too fast when asked to do a transition, he will lose balance. If he is going too slowly, he will lose the engagement of his haunches.

I.2 Go aids: the horse is being ridden forwards in rhythm.

Turn aids

Turn aids are necessary for every change of direction or bend: to negotiate a track through the woods, school your horse in an arena, or to turn towards obstacles when jumping, for example. (Photo I.3)

Being able to turn your horse in balance is essential. A bad turn will affect his ability to maintain rhythm and outline, which in turn will have a knock-on effect on any transitions you ask your horse to do.

Below
I.3 Riding a turn in trot

Circles of different sizes are so important for improving your horse's suppleness. Being able to bend your horse equally in both directions is an indication of good flexibility and balance.

Flexion and bend are essential for every school movement you do, from circles to serpentines, shoulder-in to half-pass, and so on. They are also necessary for canter work; your horse will not canter in balance on the correct lead if he can neither flex at the poll nor bend in his ribs.

All three: stop, go and turn, are vital for a dressage test or a show-jumping course, for example; they enable you to produce imaginative schooling sessions with your horse and are essential for all horse sports. Riding would be a very limited sport if you could only ride your horse in straight lines at one speed all the time!

A well-trained horse is a pleasure to ride. A horse that does not respond to your aids, however, is at best a bit stiff or inattentive; at worst he is downright dangerous!

Body Awareness

To ride effectively, you should be body aware before you get into the saddle. Simple exercises can help you to improve your posture and balance, and to communicate your aids to your horse in a coordinated manner. Most of the problems we have when we ride are down to us, the riders. If we are not balanced in the saddle, our horses have no chance!

Even the slightest difference in your position will be picked up by your horse. What may seem insignificant to you will have an effect on how your horse responds to your aids. Any inconsistency in your riding, whether you are stronger on your right side than your left, or one hand is carried higher than the other, for example, will have a profound effect on the horse's balance and outline.

Most people who have horses in their lives have no spare time to go to the gym, but incorporating some simple exercises into your daily life will make a huge difference to your riding fitness and suppleness. By being aware of every little thing about your body all the time it becomes a habit and will come naturally to you when you are riding.

Loosening-up and warming-up exercises

Many people think they should stretch before they exercise, but actually it is better to stretch when your muscles are warm, not cold. Start your day by moving around slowly for a few minutes while everything loosens up. As we get older, this does take a bit longer, but do try to get out of snail mode at some point in the day, otherwise you will never become fitter!

Even getting yourself out of bed and dressed can be used as preliminary loosening up; how many of you struggle to put your socks on in the morning because your back is stiff? Bending down suddenly to tie your boot laces is a sure-fire way to put your back out; it is easier and more muscle-friendly to put your foot up on a chair to attend to your footwear and will stretch your back muscles gently.

The time to stretch is once you are on the move, but start off gently. Give your muscles time to stretch – suddenly grabbing at your arms or legs and hauling at them is the way to pull a muscle or two. Dashing around makes your muscles tense but if you are in a hurry, try to move smoothly and build up to full speed, remembering to breathe at the same time! Muscles need oxygen to function and your joints need lubricating. Give your body a chance to get into gear before you make heavy demands on it.

Walking around the yard, taking horses to and from fields and even walking your horse around the arena before riding, is one of the best exercises to get your muscles warmed up (Photo I.4).

I.4 One of the best ways of warming up is to go for a walk. Leading your horse around the school is a good way to do this.

Below
I.5a and b a) Mucking out incorrectly: facing away from the barrow, twisting the body with a hollow back and throwing the muck on an angle; this is a sure way to get a bad back. b) Mucking out correctly: facing the barrow and throwing the muck straight in front of you.

Yard tasks

At the yard, start off with tasks that are easier on your back such as feeding horses and leading them to the field. Then you can proceed with the heavier work such as mucking out and carrying water buckets about. As you work, be aware of your breathing and the way you move around. Do you, for example, stoop forwards when you walk or carry things more in one hand than the other? (Photos I.5a and b, and I.6a and b)

Grooming your horse can be a good workout in itself. Applying pressure as you brush him is good for toning your arms; bending down to pick his feet out and to brush his legs is good for your leg and back strength. Relax and breathe as you groom, you will enjoy the experience as much as your horse!

I.6a and b a) Picking up water buckets incorrectly with a rounded back. b) Picking up water buckets correctly with a straight back.

Posture and fitness

If you feel stiff when you are about to ride, then your horse will not be able to give his best. Be aware of any old injuries you have that may cause a problem. Notice if you have one arm or leg weaker or stronger than the other, or if you naturally stand with more weight on one leg than the other. Check your posture in a mirror before you start – see if your shoulders are level and your hips are straight. Have a look from the front and the side (Photo I.7).

A brisk walk with the dog or leading your horse to the field will increase your breathing rate. Once you have deposited your horse into his field, swinging your arms as you walk back to the stables will get your circulation going. Up your mucking-out speed a bit as you get into the swing of it, and try to use your stomach muscles as you shovel and sweep – this beats doing loads of sit-ups! (Photo I.8)

Stretching exercises

Here are some ideas for stretching your muscles. We will start from the head and work downwards.

Neck stretches

Having a stiff neck can affect your head and shoulder posture. It is also a sign of tension, and often goes together with clenching your jaw. Your horse will mirror what you do but, so often, a rider will not take their own posture into considera-

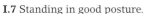

I.7 Standing in good posture.

Right
I.8 Sweeping correctly is good aerobic exercise. If it is done correctly with a bit of effort, your breathing and heart rate will increase!

tion but complain that their horse is tight in the jaw, or in his poll. The simplest solution – and this should be the first thing to try rather than changing the bit, noseband or resorting to gadgets – is for the rider to simply relax their jaw and neck. Here are a few simple neck exercises to try.

- Stand tall, with your feet hip-width apart; let your arms hang by your sides and have your head central, facing forwards. Lower your chin towards your chest and then raise it until you are looking up to the sky or ceiling – depending on where you are! Repeat this slowly a few times. (Photos I.9a and b)

I.9a and b Neck exercise a) Raising the chin and (b) lowering it again stretches the front and back of the neck.

- Stand in good posture with your head central, facing the front. Turn your head to the right as far as you can comfortably go without forcing it. Then turn your head to the left. Repeat about four times each way. Finish the exercise with your head facing to the front again. (Photos I.10a and b)

- Stand in good posture, with your head central, facing the front. Now, tilt your head to the right, lowering your right ear to your right shoulder. Make sure you do not lift your shoulder up towards your ear. Return the head to the central upright position momentarily before repeating to the left. Do this about four times each way. Finish the exercise with your head upright. (Photos I.11a and b)

- Once again, stand in good posture, with your head central, facing the front. Turn your head so you are looking up high to the right. Rotate your head, letting your chin describe the movement: lower your chin towards your chest, then take it across your chest until you are looking up to the left. Repeat about four times, travelling right to left and then left to right. This exercise helps to release tension in your neck. Keep your jaw relaxed – no teeth clenching! (Photos I.12a–c)

Top row
I.10a and b Turning the head right (a) and left (b) to mobilise the neck.

Bottom row
I.11a and b Tilting the head taking the ear to the shoulder, right (a) and then to the left (b).

I.12a–c Rotating the head to release neck tension.

Rib stretches

If you tend to lean to one side when you are standing on the ground, it is most likely that you do the same in the saddle. Keeping your ribcage lifted will help counter this and also aids breathing, which in turn helps you to relax. Stretching up through the ribs is a great way to mobilise your upper body and make you feel tall and proud – it's a fantastic feeling when you ride like this!

I.13 Stretching up through the ribs.

- Stand tall with your right arm stretched up and your left arm across your front with your hand on your ribs.

- Reach up a little more with your right arm and feel your ribs lifting on your right side, and then lower your arm down by your side again. As you do this, try to keep your ribs lifted. (Photo I.13)

- Repeat with your left arm raised and your right hand on your ribs.

Shoulder loosening

Tension in the shoulders is very common amongst riders. This has the knock-on effect of making the rein contact tense. So many horses will work much more happily and in a correct outline once the rider has relaxed their shoulders!

- Lift both shoulders as far as you can and lower them again, keeping your neck stretched and your head straight. (Photos I.14a and b)

- Circle each shoulder in turn, Raise them to start with, and then rotate them backwards. Be aware of your shoulder blades moving together as you move your shoulder backwards, and then moving apart as you bring your shoulder forwards again. (Photos I.15a–c)

- Rotate one elbow at a time in a circle to the rear. Raise the elbow to shoulder height, lift the elbow and then circle it back and down to the starting position. Repeat a few times with each arm. (Photos I.16a–d)

- Circle both elbows to the rear at the same time. This makes the shoulder roll more difficult and requires more muscle strength than just rolling your shoulders. Raise both elbows to shoulder height, lift them and circle them back and down to the starting position. Repeat a few times with each arm. (Photos I.17a–d, see overleaf)

Hip loosening

If your hips are tight, firstly you will have a problem mounting your horse and, secondly, the tightness will prevent your horse's back from moving correctly. Loose hips allow the movement of the horse's back to happen. A bonus is that you will walk better on your own two feet if your hip joints are able to move properly!

- Stand in good posture with your hands on your hips and keeping your shoulders back and down. Circle your hips by moving the hips to the right, then push

I.14a and b Lift and lower your shoulders.

I.15a–c Lifting and circling the shoulders.

Below
I.16a–d Rotate one elbow in a circle to the rear, back, and down, returning to the start position in front.

I.17a–d Rotate both elbows in a circle to the rear, back, and down, returning to the start position in front.

them backwards, move them to the left, and then push them forwards. Start the circles to the right a few times, and then to the left. Keep your knee and ankle joints soft so that they can move also, which will co-ordinate the movement of all your leg joints in one circling motion. (Photos I.18a–e, see opposite)

Leg stretches

We all dream of having lovely long legs – both on and off the horse! The way to maximise your leg length is to stretch your leg muscles. This also helps you to keep weight into your stirrups; drawing the legs up when giving leg aids is a common fault in riders. A short, tight leg position creates tension in the hips, and affects the upper body posture, with the rider invariably crouching forwards in a very insecure riding position. Keeping the legs down into the stirrups is much more secure. This also applies to the jumping position – the weight can still be down into the lower leg even with shorter stirrups.

- Place one of your feet forwards, and the other behind you with the feet one stride's width apart. Keeping your weight evenly on both feet, slowly bend your front knee. This creates a stretch down the back of the straight leg – be aware of your calf muscles lengthening as you do this. It is important to ease yourself into this stretch position and not to do it suddenly. Repeat on the other leg.

I.18a–e Stand in good posture. Circle the hips – first to the right and then to the left – allowing your knees and ankles to rotate also.

- Place your feet apart with your feet turned slightly out in a comfortable position, about as wide apart as a natural step to the side. Bend one knee forward over the toe of the same foot so that the muscles on the inside of the other leg are stretched. Repeat the other way.

- Stand with your hands on your hips with your feet parallel and hip-width apart. and stretch one leg out in front of you. This can be either with your toe pointed, or raised with your ankle flexed (this exercise is easier to do if you have your riding boots on). Then put your foot back flat on the ground. Stretch your leg to the side and replace, then to the rear and replace. Repeat with the other leg. This stretches all the muscles in your legs. (Photos I.19a–c)

I.19a–c Stretch one leg out in front of you, then to the side and behind. Repeat the exercise with the other leg.

Opposite, below
I.21a and b a) Standing with the hands on the hips in preparation for waist bends. b) Waist bends to the right. Repeat to the left.

Spine stretches

A healthy back is essential for riding. Correct posture in the saddle can improve back strength and mobility such a lot. The more supple your back is, the better you will ride! Stretching your arms straight up above your head will lengthen your spine. Stretching to one side and then the other will bend your whole spine in both directions.

I.20 Raise both arms overhead. From this position, stretch alternate arms upwards (Lorraine's arms are straight, correctly so, but mine are bent, and not fully extended.)

- Stretching up tall, alternately reaching up with one arm and then the other will lengthen your spine. Note if you can stretch more easily on one side than the other. Practise a few times each side until you feel evenly stretched on both sides. Imagine increasing the space between your hips and your ribs. You can either have the palms of your hands facing forwards, or facing each other. Once you have stretched up as far as you can, lower your arms by your sides without collapsing your upper body – you should feel a few inches taller! (Photo I.20)

- Stand with your hands on your hips. Bend the upper body to the side from the waist without twisting, so you are stretching through your ribs as you bend sideways. Keep your weight even on both feet to keep your balance. Repeat the other side and then repeat a few times on both sides. (Photos I.21a and b)

a

b

Hand stretches

What you do with your hands when you ride is so important. Maintaining a steady, elastic contact is very dependent on your hand position, and the placement of each finger. The horse feels in his mouth, via the bit, how tightly or loosely you are holding the reins. Tension in your hands can also transfer to your forearms and shoulders. If your horse is unsettled with the contact, the first thing to check is that your hand position is steady without gripping with your fingers or tightening your wrists.

- With your hands in riding position, clench your fists, and release again. As you do this, you may feel your shoulders and forearms tighten. Release the tension in your hands and feel your shoulders and arms relax. (Photos I.22a and b)

- Circle your wrists in both directions. Notice if you have one wrist stiffer than the other. Repeat the circling a few times. (Photos I.23a–d)

- Press the palms of your the hands together, and then your fingers, giving them a good stretch. Peel your hands away again, palms first then fingers. Repeat a few times.

- Clench your fists tightly with your fingers pressed together. Then open your hand and spread your fingers wide apart to give them a really good stretch. (Photos I.24a and b)

To finish this set of hand exercises, stand in riding position with your hands correctly placed in front of you with your elbows by your sides. Your hands should feel much more relaxed after doing the exercises, and you should be more aware of any tension creeping in when you ride. (Photo I.25, see overleaf)

I.22a and b a) A correctly closed fist with the fingers relaxed and the thumb slightly bent. b) A tightly clenched fist; note how tense the forearm becomes. The thumb is pressed firmly down onto the first finger.

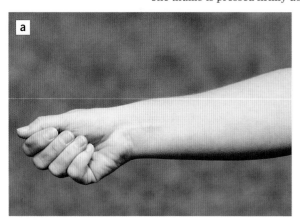

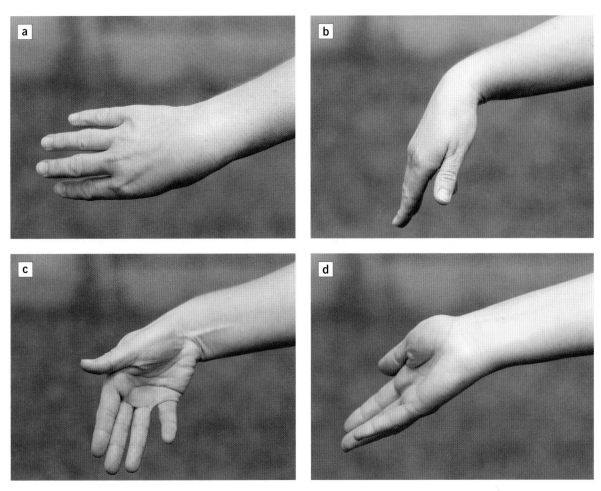

1.23a–d Move your hands in a circle to loosen your wrists.

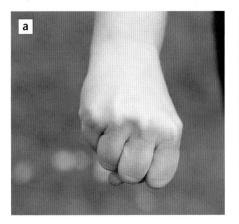

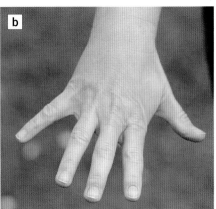

I.24a and b a) Clench your fist tightly with your fingers pressed together, and then (b) stretch your fingers as far apart as you can.

I.25 To finish this set of hand exercises, stand in riding position with your hands correctly placed in front of you with your elbows by your sides.

Rider Exercises for Stop, Go, Turn

Stop

Stopping is all about body control. To ask your horse to halt, you must be able to hold your position really still and maintain your balance equally on both feet. You must keep your upper body upright with your shoulders square, your elbows by your sides and your hands parallel. Your hands must not pull back or fiddle with the reins. Tipping forwards or backwards will unsettle your horse, and he will not be able to stand still. This is the 'neutral' position and you need to learn where neutral is when you are standing on the ground in riding position.

Shoulder exercises

In order to halt, it is important to maintain good shoulder posture with your shoulders back and down, which will have a beneficial effect on your arm and hand position, and the contact with the horse's mouth. Keeping your shoulder blades pressed down and back maintains tone in your upper back muscles. This is important for remaining upright at all times – especially if your horse has developed the habit of pulling at the reins when you ask him to stop.

- Place your arms in a low V. Press your shoulder blades back and together, and release. Repeat a few times. (Photos I.26a and b)

- Stretch both arms out in front of you. Open both arms out to the side in line with your body, then bring them back to shoulder width apart again. (Photos I.27a and b)

I.26a and b Press the shoulder blades back and together.

I.27a and b Open the arms out to the side and bring them back to shoulder width apart.

- With your arms out to the sides, in line with your shoulders, bend your arms from the elbows so both hands are pointing upwards. Raise both arms at the same time, stretching your finger tips to the sky, and lower again so your elbows are in line with your shoulders. (Photos I.28a and b)

- Press your shoulder blades together with your arms raised to shoulder height and bent at the elbows, in the same position as in Photos I.28a and b. This is a stronger version of the previous shoulder blade press.

Hip exercises

When you ask your horse to stop, it is important to make sure your hips are upright at all times. With the hips upright, you will be sitting on both seat bones. This position ensures that your core muscles – the muscles in the middle of your back and your stomach muscles – are engaged holding you upright. Using your core muscles also makes your arm and leg aids very effective for little effort. Keeping your hips upright requires toned lumbar – 'jeans back-pockets' – muscles, and abdominals. Once you are aware of all these muscles, you will be amazed how effective your hip (seat) aids can be!

- Place your hands on your hips with your feet hip-width apart. Stick your backside out behind you, hollowing your back. You will feel your lower back muscles tighten, and your stomach muscles slacken. This is one example of poor posture. (Photo I.29)

- Now tighten your abdominal muscles, and bring your hips to an upright position. Your back and stomach muscles should work equally to maintain this posture – this is the correct position for riding and walking. Now tuck your backside under. This slackens your back muscles, and tightens your stomach. Your chest will drop, and your chest will cave in. This is another example of poor posture (Photo I.30).

- Practise sticking your backside out, bringing your hips upright and then tucking your backside under a few times. This is known as a 'pelvic tilt' exercise, which is very good for learning awareness of your hip position.

You need to be able to hold an upright hip position to be able to stop properly! (Photos I.31a and b)

Balancing exercise

Keeping your balance central in the saddle is essential for a square halt. Keeping your weight correctly balanced on your feet in the stirrups is just as important as keeping your hips upright and sitting on both seat bones. Acquiring the feel for this is best done standing on the ground.

Above
I.28a and b Bend your arms from the elbows and raising both arms at the same time, stretch your fingers up to the sky, and then lower your arms so your elbows are in line with your shoulders again.

Far left
I.29 Hollowing the back.

Left
I.30 Rounding the back.

Below
I.31a and b a) Standing with upright hips on the ground, and (b) sitting with upright hips on the horse.

Your feet should be placed in the stirrups with the widest part of your foot on the stirrup. Your toes should be relaxed and your weight distributed evenly across all your toes (Photo I.32).

Putting weight on the balls of your feet will turn your knees in (Photo I.33). Weight on your little toes will turn your knees out (Photo I.34).

Your foot position also affects your leg position. Rolling your feet inwards places all your weight on your knees and brings your lower leg away from the horse. Rolling your feet outwards brings your thighs and knees away from the horse's sides.

Your balance will be affected by where your weight is distributed on your feet in the stirrups. This is a really good aspect to practise on the ground. Putting weight to the front of your feet will cause you to lean forwards. Putting weight into your heels will cause you to lean backwards.

Below left
I.32 Your weight should be evenly placed across the widest part of your feet.

Below centre
I.33 Putting weight on the insides of your feet, on your big toe, will cause your knees to turn in and your lower leg to come off the horse.

Below right
I.34 Putting weight on the outsides of your feet, on your little toe, will cause your knees to come away from the horse's sides.

- Stand in riding position. Begin with your weight centrally placed on both feet. Your legs will feel comfortable in riding position with your knees and ankles softly flexed. (Photo I.35, see opposite)

- Ease your weight forwards to your toes. You should feel as though you will tip forwards, losing your balance. Your heels will lift and your calf muscles tighten and shorten. (Photo I.36, see opposite)

- Now tip your weight back onto your heels. You should feel as though you will topple over backwards. Your toes will lift and the front of your thighs will tense up in an effort to stop you falling over. (Photo I.37, see opposite)

Above left
I.35 Your weight should be level on both feet and across the widest part of the foot.

Above right
I.36 Standing with the weight forwards on the toes.

Right
I.37 Standing with the weight tipped backwards on the heels.

Go

Going involves being able to synchronise your body movement with that of your horse. You need to be aware of which parts of your body should move with the horse, namely your hips and lower back, and which should not, namely your upper body and hands, in particular.

When asking your horse to go, you may need to use both legs to ask him to go forwards, or use one leg more firmly than the other to ask him to go sideways. You may need to use one leg more than the other in order to correct your horse if he is unbalanced or crooked.

Once he has found his balance, use both legs with the same pressure. If you *continually* use one leg more than the other, you will compound any crookedness issues. This can result in an uneven contact. So, if your horse holds his head to one side, it may be a result of uneven leg aids, which means you are not asking him to go in balance.

Your hips, knees and ankles must act as shock absorbers when your horse is in motion. Your upper body must remain under control and not flop around all over the place! It is important to maintain your upper body posture while allowing your hips to move with the horse's back. Your knees and ankles must also move, acting as shock absorbers of the 'spring' of the horse's strides.

Mobilisation of joints exercise

This simple exercise will help to mobilise your leg joints.

- Stand with your feet parallel and bend your knees into riding position. Place your hands on your knees. Circle your knees to the right and to the left allowing your feet and ankles to move also. (Photos I.38a–c)

Balancing exercise

This a good exercise for balancing, keeping your body weight central. Your core muscles maintain your balance. Your supporting leg must also work to keep your balance.

- Keeping your hips straight and upright, bend your knees slightly. Place your hands on your hips. Standing on your left leg, stretch your right leg out in front, and point your toes. Then raise them, pointing your heel down. This mobilises your ankle and also stretches your lower leg muscles. Alternate between moving your toes down and up. Repeat on the other leg. (Photos I.39a and b)

- Turn your right foot out to the right side, and then turn it inwards to the left. (Photo I.40a and b, see overleaf) Now circle your foot both ways. This loosens the ankle joint. Repeat with the other leg.

I.38a–c Circling the knees.

Below
I.39a and b Moving the foot up and down.

I.40a and b Turning the
foot from side to side.

Inside and outside leg muscles exercise

You will use the muscles on the inside and outside of your legs to put pressure
against the horse's sides and to release it again when giving leg aids.

- Stand with both legs parallel and your knees straight. Hold your arms outstretched at shoulder height to help you balance. Raise your right leg in front
  of you, and back down. Take it across in front of your left leg, and back again.
  Take it out to the side, and replace it. Do the same thing with your left leg.
  (Photos I.41a–c)

Turn

Before riding any turn or circle, you need to 'position' the horse to the right or left,
indicating to him what is coming next. This involves a positioning of your body to
the right or left. If you position your horse to the left, your left side is on the inside
of the bend. If you position your horse to the right, your right side is on the inside
of the bend.

 You need to turn your upper body, head, arms and hands in the direction you
wish to go. Your upper body should turn as one unit with your hips and shoulders
parallel. Your chin should be in line with the middle of your chest.

 It is important you turn from the hips as this movement relocates the whole
leg from the thigh downwards and positions your leg correctly. The correct out-
side-leg position will not be obtained by bending the leg from the knee alone.

I.41a–c a) Raise your right leg in front of you with your arms outstretched for balance. b) Take the leg across in front of you. c) Take the same leg out to the side.

This positioning will guide and ask the horse to turn with you. At the same time, you need to support him with your legs so that he can turn with you in balance. If you turn from the waist, your horse will not turn with you.

Turning your hips to the left positions your inside (left) leg by the girth, and your outside (right) leg behind the girth. Turning your hips to the right means that your inside (right) leg is by the girth, and your outside (left) leg goes behind it.

The soles of your feet should be parallel with the ground and not with your outside heel pointing skywards!

It is also important to be able to position your horse correctly for a canter strike-off to the right or left. Lateral work is dependent on correct flexion and bend and is so useful for improving suppleness and developing collection (taking weight behind) and impulsion (energy).

Opposite page, top and centre row
I.42a–d a) Stand with your arms folded in front of your chest, touching each elbow with your fingers. b) Turn to the right from your waist, keeping your arms where they are and turning your head in line with your chest. c) Extend your right arm at right angles to your body, keeping your other hand touching your right elbow. d) Bend your right elbow again so both hands are touching both elbows.

The following two exercises will help you see and feel the difference between turning from the waist and turning from the hips.

The first exercise, turning from the waist, keeping the hips still, is to help you to feel your core muscles supporting you as you turn, maintaining an upright body position. Many people tend to lean to the side as they turn, collapsing the waist, so this exercise can help you to avoid doing this. The second exercise is to turn from the hips as you should do when in the saddle. If you do not turn your hips, your horse will not turn with you!

Turning from the waist

- Stand straight with your arms folded in front of you. This arm position helps you to keep your ribs lifted and your shoulders square, and prevents any tendencies to lean to the side as you turn. Turn to the right from your waist without moving your hips. Repeat to the left. Keep your chin in line with your chest as you turn. Turn to the right from your waist again, this time extend your right arm at right angles to your body, keeping your other hand touching your right elbow. This helps you to focus forwards in the direction your shoulders are facing, and you will feel your core muscles work a little harder to support you as you extend your arm. Bend your right elbow again so both hands are touching both elbows. (Photos I.42a–d) Repeat to the left side, this time extending your left arm. This can either be done with your legs straight, hip-width apart for balance, or in riding position with the knees slightly bent. Your hips remain static in an upright position. Once you are aware of your core muscles, try the second exercise, turning from the hips, in riding position. You can also turn from the waist with your arms in riding position, but avoid leaning over!

Turning from the hips

- Stand in riding position, with your knees bent and your chin in line with your chest and turn from your hips this time, rather than your waist. Your upper body should turn as one unit from the hips. Keep your hips and shoulders parallel as you turn. You can repeat the arm positions from the first exercise, to ensure your shoulders are level and your core muscles are still engaged. Maintain your upper body position and engaged core muscles. Turning from the hips has to be done in riding position with your knees bent as your hips will not turn if your legs are locked straight.

Opposite page, bottom row
I.43a and b a) Stand in riding position. b) Turn from your hips to the right.

Then try turning from the hips with your arms in riding position with your hands remaining parallel as you turn (Photos I.43a and b).

When mounted it is important to keep your balance on both seat bones and into both stirrups when you turn: it helps the horse to keep his balance on both hind

legs as he turns. Keeping your hands parallel is also very important as it helps the horse to keep his ears level and to flex at the poll as he turns.

COMMON PROBLEMS

- **A stiff or crooked rider** creates a stiff or crooked horse!

- **Many rider problems stem from old habits or injuries**. It is all too easy to allow muscles to seize up, so crookedness becomes a habit. If this is the case, standing straight can feel awkward. If your horse becomes crooked, do check your own posture first – it can save a lot of time and vet bills if the remedy is simply to sit straighter in the saddle! If you walk with your weight more to one side, your saddle may become lopsided, and your horse may have difficulty turning one way or the other. He may favour one canter lead, especially when jumping. Lateral work may be easier one way. This could all be caused by the rider's crookedness.

- **A stiff inflexible back** may result in a rider having difficulty sitting to the trot. The horse might then be blamed for having a stiff back, or an 'extravagant' movement that is hard to sit to. Unless the rider can use their back properly to encourage proper back movement in the horse, this problem will not go away. There is nothing better than riding a horse with a supple back but this can only be achieved by a supple rider!

Self-awareness

Relaxation

When you are riding, you can tell if your horse is relaxed because he will lower his neck, swing his back, chew the bit, and most importantly, breathe deeply and regularly. He will snort to clear his airways, and you will feel his ribcage expand and contract as he breathes in and out.

The most effective way of relaxing yourself when you ride is to regulate *your* breathing. Breathe steadily in and out, and be aware of the air flowing in and out of your lungs. Horses communicate by sniffing and blowing to each other and so if your horse can hear you breathing, you are communicating with him.

Make sure you can move every part of your body with mobile joints; if anything is 'stuck', if, for example, your fingers feel stiff, then you are tense. Take a few moments to do a head-to-toe check on yourself to eliminate any adverse tension in your body. This does not mean flopping around: muscle tone (positive tension) is necessary for body control and suppleness. (Photo I.44)

I.44 A happy and relaxed horse and rider.

Positive mental attitude

The most important aspect of horsemanship, including handling as well as riding, is to maintain a positive mental attitude at all times. This is easier said than done I know, but it is the only way to get the best from your horse.

Fear clutters the brain: a 'busy brain' focuses on the 'what ifs': What if my horse spooks at that bird? What if I fall off? What if I lose my stirrups? And so on. Does this sound familiar? Try to switch off these negative buttons in your mind.

Trying too hard does not work either; forceful thoughts such as: 'Get in that trailer, you old ****', or 'Get over that jump, or else!' create tension by putting the horse under too much mental pressure. The best way to deal with things is to have a quiet mind; this means just staying in the here and now and ditching the everyday mental chatter that can go on in your head. With a quiet, clear mind you are able to give your horse mental instructions; believe me, horses do pick these up!

To achieve this stillness of thought, you have to be aware of all your senses – what can you see, hear, and smell?

You must believe in both your own ability and that of your horse for him to trust you and to try for you. He must be able to look to you as a friend who will look out for him in every situation. (Photo I.45)

I.45 A positive attitude gives you a good bond with your horse. Try to stay focused at all times.

COMMON PROBLEMS

- **Holding your breath and tensing** will make your horse become tense and he will breathe shallowly. If your body becomes tight and you feel unable to move and you cannot relax yourself, your horse will most probably find his own way of releasing tension by spooking. Being a flight animal, the horse's natural response to fear is to run away. This then frightens the rider, who becomes tense, and then the horse becomes more afraid.

- **A negative mental attitude** will have an adverse effect on your horse. Over time, he will lose confidence in you and no longer trust you. His confidence and trust is vital in situations where he will look to you as herd leader for guidance, when you may meet heavy traffic on the road, or are at a busy competition venue, for example. A good illustration of the right mental attitude is the Olympic Games equestrian competitions; it was amazing to see how focused all the riders were at such a tremendous event. If a rider had lost faith in their horse even for a split second, the outcome could have been a lost medal!

- **If you are not in the right frame of mind for riding** when you are with your horse; you may have had a bad day at work or a hectic schedule, or the weather is particularly horrid, for example, then it is better to just spend time with your horse and calm down. Give him a good groom, clean your tack, or work him from the ground. There is always tomorrow!

STOP

The Importance of the Halt

The importance of being able to stop is (hopefully) obvious! Many people have their first ride on holiday with horses following each other in a line, with little, if any, knowledge about how to control the horses. They may have been given crude instructions such as 'pull the reins to stop, and kick to go'. Well, they say ignorance is bliss!

In these circumstances, if the rider is relaxed, then the horse will go quietly with his friends. If the rider is tense, however, it is a totally different ball game: the horse's flight instinct kicks in, the rider becomes more anxious, the horse then runs faster or spooks, and the rider falls off. I meet many people who have 'had a go' at riding in this way, only to be put off going near a horse at all in the future, having been left with the impression that horses are nasty things that bite, kick and throw you off.

I think the first thing any rider should learn is how to stop. So many accidents happen because riders have no control over their horses. When you learn to drive a car, the first thing you are shown is where the brake pedal is – no-one in their right mind would drive a car if they were not familiar with the controls, and certainly not if the brakes did not work!

So why is it important to be able to stop? If when riding on the road you come to a road junction and your horse won't stand still, you are in danger of having a serious accident with a vehicle. Or you may be hacking out and your horse might spook at either something in the hedge or a noisy vehicle. Some instructors may tell you to 'kick on' and 'ride your horse forwards' out of the situation but I think this just winds the horse up and you probably end up worse off than if you just stopped in the first place. Developing an automatic reflex to halt if your horse becomes frightened will get you out of all sorts of trouble. Stopping can give you thinking time to work out how best to get to safety.

If when jumping fences in a show-jumping arena, or across country, you cannot stop in case of emergency – if you are on totally the wrong stride for take-off, for example – you can avoid landing in a heap of poles, or head first into a ditch, by being able to stop before the jump!

In a dressage test, a correct, square halt can clock up a good number of marks for a competitor but, even at the top levels of dressage, many riders can't halt and their horses won't stand still even for a second.

So if you want to do well in any aspect of riding, learn how to halt. (Photos 1.1a and b)

1.1a and b a) A square halt in a correct outline with the rider in a balanced, upright position in the saddle. b) A poor halt in a hollow outline. The horse has lifted his neck and dipped his back, becoming hollow, and one hind leg is trailing a little.

Stopping in balance

The aim of correct halts and half-halts is to balance the horse with a rider on board and if he is balanced, i.e. in 'four-wheel drive' and in self-carriage, not on his fore-hand and leaning on the reins, he is easy to stop.

In this section, I will explain how to ride halts and half-halts to help your horse to balance while carrying a rider. The horse is naturally built with his weight more on the front end than the back end and so to prevent the horse from carrying the extra weight of the rider on his forehand as well, he has to be taught to take weight on his haunches.

How to Ride the Perfect Halt

So how do you ride a perfect halt? Most people's instinctive reaction is to pull on the reins and expect the horse to stop, but in actual fact, this is the worst thing to do. A nasty pull in the mouth may make the horse stop by hurting him, but he will not stand still in a relaxed manner. As soon as you release the contact he will most likely run away as his flight instinct kicks in. Hanging on to the contact may make you feel in control but in reality the more you pull, the more the horse will become tense and anxious. To ride a perfect halt, you must use your whole body.

1.2 A correct hand position when holding the reins, with the elbows by the sides. The fingers could be closed around the reins a little more.

How to ask your horse to stop

The halt aid is basically a 'body block': if you stop, so does your horse. This can only be achieved if you have a correct position in the saddle.

Let's start from the head and work downwards. First of all you have to sit up nice and tall in the saddle, looking straight ahead. Keeping your chest up and your shoulders straight and level, press your shoulder blades together bringing your upper arms close by your sides in contact with your body. There should be no daylight between the side seams of your clothing and your elbows, though they should not be clamped tightly into your body, just touching.

Carry your hands in front of you, bit-width apart, placed either side of the pommel of the saddle. I often explain this as holding a tea tray. Your thumbs should point slightly towards each other: point your right thumb to the horse's left ear, and your left thumb to his right ear. The position of your hands should not change when you ask your horse to halt; do not pull back, simply keep them in the same place all the time. (Photo 1.2)

Aids for the halt

Close your legs against your horse's sides, utilising the thighs, knees and calves together. Sit still and brace your back by tightening your core muscles (stomach and back muscles) and keep your hips upright. Your thighs will lift the horse's back, your knees will stop forward movement, and your calves will bring his hind legs under his back end. You need to apply sufficient 'squeeze' to be effective: the more balanced the horse, the less pressure will be needed.

Increasing your muscle tone blocks the horse's back movement. If you think of stopping yourself, you will stop the horse. A very responsive horse will stop if you just tighten your core muscles but firmer leg aids and rein contact are needed if the horse needs support.

If you need a firm rein aid, you must counter-balance this with firm legs. The reins must never be firmer than your legs or back aids.

Once your horse has responded to your aids and stopped, you need to release the aids by just softening your muscles a little without collapsing your core muscles. If you collapse, you are not maintaining your own halt position and your horse is likely to move again before you have fully established the halt. It is important, therefore, to stay in your halt position, maintaining a braced back until he stands still in balance with a soft rein contact.

A test of a good halt is to allow the horse to stretch his head and neck all the way down to the ground on a loose rein. He should do this without moving his feet!

How to achieve a square halt and why

The horse should stand square, which means that his body weight is equally distributed over all four legs. The front and hind legs should form the corners of a rectangle (it's not actually a true square) with the hind legs under the pelvis, – not left out behind as is often seen. The horse is designed like a suspension bridge, with his neck and back supported by his legs. He should be able to stand still in balance, maintaining the halt without you having to hang on to him, i.e. if you soften the rein contact he should remain standing still.

The timing of your halt aid is very important. Asking at the wrong moment will make your horse unbalanced and the halt will not be precise. Any aids should be given in the rhythm of the gait you are in. For instance, the preparation could be to count 1, 2, 3, halt to correspond with the individual rhythms of the walk, trot or canter.

Aids given out of rhythm will surprise the horse, and result in tension, which is not conducive to a balanced, relaxed halt.

It is very important to sit straight, maintain an even contact on both reins, equal contact with both legs and sit with your weight equally placed on both seat bones. If you load one side of the horse's back more than the other, or pull his head to one side, causing crookedness, he will not be able to halt straight. (Photos 1.3a and b) You can, therefore, have a square halt that is not straight. In a dressage test, for a competitor to achieve top marks the halt must be both square and straight. You can also have a straight halt that is not square where one hind leg is left behind.

It should be possible to ride an accurate, square halt from walk, trot or canter, though this is easier said than done! Make sure you can halt from a walk before attempting from trot. Once you have achieved trot to halt, if your canter work is balanced and you can ride the transitions trot/canter/trot and walk/canter/walk, then you could try canter to halt. Take things step by step – any transition issues should be tackled first. (See Half-halts on page 52)

If your aids are correct but your horse cannot stand square, if, for example, he fidgets around, or continually places his hind legs wide apart, or his front legs too close together, then he may need more physical strength to be able to stand still. Alternatively, he may need to be mentally more trusting of the rider, otherwise his flight instinct will kick in again. A square halt is an indication of a well-trained horse.

Other factors that can affect the horse's ability to halt squarely are pain or discomfort and weak muscles. If the horse is poorly schooled and does not have correct muscle development, he may not be able to sustain a halt. A halt must have 'immobility'; in other words, the horse must be able to stand still calmly, not – as often seen – pausing momentarily before shuffling off, often crookedly. From a square halt, the horse should move off straight and not to one side or the other.

1.3a and b The only way to achieve a square halt is to sit in a good position. a) A good riding position. b) A bad riding position with rounded shoulders and back.

Half-halts

Half-halts explained

What is a half-halt? The textbook description is: 'A simultaneous action of the rider's seat, leg and rein aids bringing the horse into balance by encouraging him to take weight behind'. It is the most important aid of all in riding as it has such a dramatic effect on the horse's whole way of going, but it is so often misinterpreted and not understood.

A well-timed half-halt is a reflex-action response by the rider to the horse's need for the slightest rebalancing requiring split-second timing.

The half-halt, or rather a series of half-halts, helps to balance the horse and tells him to step under behind, i.e. to tuck his pelvis and bring his hind legs underneath him, which helps him to use his back in the right way and thus to work properly under the rider. Many riders think a half-halt is achieved with the reins but, as with the halt – the half-halt is in fact half a halt – it is achieved with a body aid.

When do we use half-halts?

Half-halts ensure that you have your horse's attention. If he is distracted for whatever reason, your half-halts will need to be firm enough to get a response from him. Once you get a correct reaction from him, you can use more subtle ones. A really responsive horse will respond to just a tightening of your stomach muscles. As stated above, the effect of series of half-halts is to balance the horse so he is more able to respond to the rider's aids. When you are riding your horse, whether you are in a schooling session, jumping a course of jumps, or hacking out, you should use hundreds of half-halts to maintain his attention and balance throughout. Half-halts keep you safe by ensuring you have full control over your horse at all times.

How to ride a half-halt

As mentioned earlier, many riders think that you stop the horse with the reins. The same riders are under the impression that tugging on the reins is the way to ask for half-halts. I always ask these riders, 'How on earth does twiddling with the reins ask the horse to take weight behind?' The half-halt tells the horse to step under behind, and it is not achieved by fiddling with the reins!

Aids for the half-halt

To ask for a half-halt, sit in the correct position and use your body in the same way as when asking your horse to halt but, unlike the halt, the stop is only momentary. You need to increase your muscle tone to body block the horse, to prevent him from moving forwards.

Maintain your hand position and a steady contact with the bit. Sit up tall, brace your back to bring his hind legs under his body, and close your legs to hold your horse. Press your shoulder blades together and close your elbows to your sides. This increase of body tone will 'press' the horse into the contact, so it will momentarily feel slightly firmer. It is very important not to pull back with your hands. Your rein contact should not be firmer than your body or you will create resistance, which your horse will either lean against, or avoid by raising his head and hollowing his back.

As you feel your horse hesitate as he responds to your stop aid, soften your muscle tone a little, release the pressure with your legs and back, and slightly soften the rein contact, just enough to allow him to move forwards. When you soften the rein contact, it is important to maintain a light feel with the bit. If the reins go loose, you have no contact, and you will lose the connection between the horse's back end and the front end. Move with your back and hips to allow him to move.

The whole action is a bit like hitting the pause button on a DVD player, and then immediately hitting 'play' again. This hesitation causes the horse to take weight behind and to push off from his hind legs as he moves forwards again. So, if you tell your horse to 'Stop, Go' in this way, he will step under behind. This makes him lighter in your hands, which enables you to soften your rein contact and allow the horse to move forwards from your hips.

Once you release the half-halt, the reins should be straight but as soft as possible – the rein contact has nothing to do with how many kilos are in your hands. Horses like to be secure in a steady contact, not one that is coming and going.

You may need to make several half-halts in succession, until the horse finds his balance and takes his weight behind. Once he does, you will feel him remain in his balance and outline. You will feel that you do not need the reins any more as they have done their job.

A good test of balance, achieved by many half-halts, is to release the reins forwards, taking your hands forwards in the direction of the bit for two or three strides (of walk, trot, or canter) before returning them to their position just in front of the pommel of the saddle, either side of the withers. This 'give and retake the reins' is a common movement in dressage tests, and is so often done incorrectly, with the rider taking their hands forwards to the horse's ears, and not releasing the contact at all.

Why do we need half-halts?

The influence of half-halts on the horse is, in effect, clutch control. If you are driving your car slowly up a hill, you will need to engage and disengage the clutch in order to stay in a low gear. To slow your horse down, you need to use frequent half-halts to keep him steady with his weight behind. As we have mentioned before, you do not slow the horse by hanging onto the reins; you must hold him with your back and legs.

Half-halts prepare the horse to make a transition from one gait to another, or within the gait when collecting and extending. For example, the horse must first take weight behind in collection before using the generated power to extend. If you ask the horse to extend without first using half-halts to set him up, he will simply run faster.

Taking Weight Behind

You may have heard the expression 'to lighten the forehand'. In essence, this is the preparation for asking your horse to stop, go or turn: his back end goes down and his front end comes up making steering easier. This is primarily achieved by riding frequent transitions, halts and, in particular, half-halts.

How does the horse take weight behind?

What happens to a horse's body when taking weight behind? The action has to start from the back end. There is no point in artificially lifting the horse's neck and head to give the impression that he is up in front. Raising his head with your hands will not affect his back end at all; in fact this will have a detrimental effect. With his head forced up, he will lock down his back, push his hind legs out behind and become tight through his shoulders. (Photo 1.4) Horses put into this false outline are often 'pushed' with a strong seat and legs to make them go forwards and are branded lazy or backwards through no fault of their own. This is in my mind downright cruel and has nothing to do with building a harmonious relationship with your horse.

As the horse takes weight behind, he tucks his pelvis under. This tightens the nuchal ligament running all along the horse's top line, from his ears to his tail. As the pelvis tucks, the loins lift. The abdominal muscles pull the hind legs under the body, and support the back from underneath. The joints of each hind leg from the croup, (lumbosacral joint) hip, stifle, hock, fetlock and pastern

1.4 Although the horse's hind feet are parallel in this photo they are not under the haunches or taking weight.

concertina, causing the lowering effect of the haunches. The hind feet step under the haunches, taking the weight of the rear end. It is this lowering effect of the haunches that gives the *impression* that the forehand has lifted; it does not actually come up.

The horse's neck arches forwards and upwards from the withers, with the poll the highest point. The nose should be on the vertical if the horse's top-line muscles are properly under the correct tension. This positive tension creates muscle tone, creating presence and *joie de vivre*. This looks totally different from a stressed horse in a false outline in the wrong balance. It should be blatantly obvious, even to a non-horsey person, from the horse's expression and demeanour if the horse is being ridden well or not.

A correctly ridden horse should be mouthing the bit in a relaxed manner, with a slight white froth around the lips as he salivates. Some horses naturally have more dribble than others. It is the rider's responsibility to be aware *at all times* if the horse is happy in his mouth. Some horses have habits that are difficult, though not impossible, to cure, such as sticking the tongue out to one side, bringing the tongue over the bit, or grinding the teeth. Though the latter is a sign of tension, some horses do this when concentrating, rather than out of resistance, but is up to the discerning rider to recognise the traits of their own horse, and to work diligently on improving the horse's balance and acceptance of the contact with frequent half-halts. There is nothing wrong with the odd sugar lump or mouthful of grass to help the horse to relax in his mouth.

Rider Posture and its Influence on Aids for Halt and Half-halts

The best way to check that your position is correct on the horse is to rehearse it on the ground. First of all, stand in good posture with your feet hip-width apart and look straight ahead. Press your shoulder blades down and back. Hold your hands in riding position. Breathe and relax. If you are tense standing still on the ground, there is not a lot of hope for you on the horse! Your muscles have to have positive tension for you to stand up, otherwise you would just be a heap of flesh and bones. Remember too that you do not need any negative mental tension.

Core muscles (stomach and back)

Be aware of your upper 'tummy' muscles, (rectus abdominus) under your breast-bone, and the middle of your back. Now take notice of your side muscles (obliques) both front and back. Tighten your lower stomach muscles (abdominals), and at the same tighten your lower back muscles (lumbar muscles). These are your core muscles which support you so you have to keep them tight. This is your stop aid from the waist up. These core muscles are vital for controlling the horse and are also the support mechanism for his front end. (Photos 1.5a–f) Imagine your upper body – above the waist – supports the front end of the horse, and your lower body – including the legs – supports the back end.

Core-muscle exercises

Opposite page
1.5a–f a) The upper tummy muscles (rectus abdominus) are the top of the core muscles on the front of your body. b) The side muscles (obliques) on the front of your body act as pillars to keep you straight. c) The abdominal muscles control your hip position from the front. d) The core muscles in your back just under your shoulder blades. e) The side muscles of your back control your back movement. f) The lumbar muscles control your hip position from the back.

- Stand in riding position and place your hands, as though you were holding the reins, under a convenient fence rail. If you are indoors, a kitchen work top will do, or a table. Brace your back and tighten your stomach muscles, and press your hands up against the underside of the fence rail or table. Imagine you are trying to lift the fence/table. As you do this, you will feel your weight increases into your feet, pressing downwards onto the ground. Keep your feet parallel with your toes relaxed. Try to lift from your stomach and not by tensing your shoulders. Try to lift the rail with your whole body – not your hands. Relax again, so you are increasing and decreasing your muscle tone. This tightening and releasing of muscle tone is isometric exercise which is very good for general body tone!

- A good way of strengthening your core muscles is to do some sit-ups. Lie on your back on the ground with your knees bent. You can do sit-ups either with your hands behind your head, or extending your arms alongside your hips –

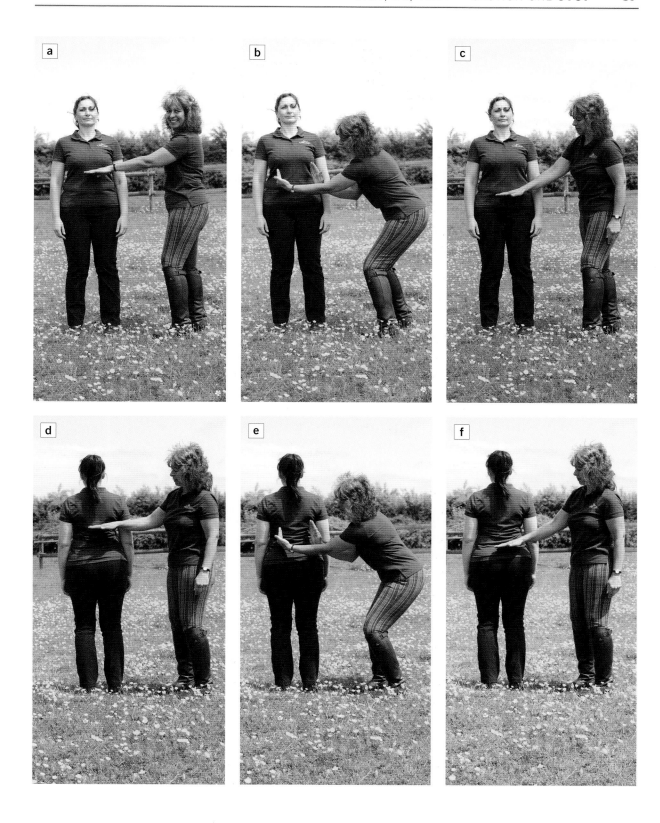

whichever you prefer. The important thing is to raise your upper body by tightening your stomach muscles and not to cheat and raise your head with your hands! (Photos 1.6a–d)

- One-sided sit-ups help to strengthen your side, or oblique, muscles. Raise one shoulder off the ground, and reach towards the opposite knee with your hand. Repeat on both sides. (Photos 1.7a and b)

1.6a–d a) Lie on the ground with your knees bent and your hands behind your head. b) Raise your upper body by tightening your tummy muscles. Make sure you are not lifting your head with your hands. c) Lower your upper body keeping control with your tummy muscles. d) Another version is to raise your upper body off the ground with your arms extended either side of your hips.

1.7a and b One-sided sit-ups work your side muscles, or obliques. a) Raise your right shoulder off the ground, reaching your hand towards your left knee. b) Raise your left shoulder off the ground, reaching your left hand towards your right knee.

Hip and leg position

Bend your knees into riding position. Make sure your knees are in line with your toes. Keep your feet flat on the floor. Put your hands on your hips – on the side seams of your trousers. The sides of your pelvis must stay upright, whether you are stationary or in motion with your horse.

Bracing the back and legs

Tighten your leg muscles to hold your position. Feel how much muscle tone you need to keep everything in place – and this is without the horse! This becomes apparent with the fence-rail exercise above.

Weight aids

Firstly stand in neutral with your weight evenly distributed between your toes and heels, and evenly on both feet. Feel how balanced and secure you feel. If you now take your weight forwards over your toes you will feel as though you are going to topple over forwards. Your back will tend to hollow and if you were on a horse you would drop the rein contact. Now take your weight back over your heels; you will feel as though you are going to fall over backwards and your instinct will be to collapse your core muscles and, again, if you were on a horse, to pull on the reins to keep your balance.

When you are in the saddle, it's important to keep your weight down into your stirrups, on the balls of your feet to stabilise the stirrup irons. Forget the idea of pushing your heels down because this puts too much weight to the back of your feet, and your stirrups will shoot forwards, which will make you collapse and sit back in the saddle. On the contrary, if you raise your heels, this puts too much weight on your toes and causes the stirrups to shoot backwards, tipping your weight forwards in the saddle.

The effect of tight and relaxed seat muscles

It is very important to keep your seat muscles relaxed at all times, which some find very difficult to achieve.

So many riders tighten their seat muscles when they are trying to stop their horses but a tight seat usually has the opposite effect: as the horse feels the seat muscles clench, he is far more likely to dip his back and go faster to get away from this nasty tight thing on his back!

Many riders are not taught to keep a close contact with their thighs. Turning the knees out brings the thighs away from the saddle, leaving daylight under the knees. The seat muscles clench and the hip joints become seized, so the rider loses all flexibility in the hips. This 'open' leg position is often accompanied by the rider sticking their toes out, and giving leg aids, not with the whole leg, but solely by jabbing with the heels. The horse, of course, resents this and is often unfairly blamed for a lack of response when in actual fact all he needs is a rider with a better seat! By sitting with the hips straight, the thighs in close contact with the saddle and the kneecaps pointing forwards, the rider is able to use all of their legs, not just the calves.

You need to practise closing your legs against the horse, using the thighs, knees and the upper calves, just under the knee area, and softening the pressure. You also need to practise using the calves to ask the horse to go, closing the thighs to lift the horse's back, and increasing the contact against the saddle with the knees as emergency brakes. A combination of all these leg aids will cover all eventualities: asking your horse to stop, go and turn, and every variation thereof!

Hand and arm position

Pressing your shoulder blades back and down and stretching across your collarbones keeps your upper arm in a good position. It is important to use your biceps muscle to keep your arm in place.

Hand and arm exercises on the ground

- Using a rope, either held by a handy friend, or attached to a fence, establish a contact on the rope and then practise softening the contact by relaxing the arms without dropping the contact. (Photos 1.8a and b)

- Standing in the riding position, bend your arms from your elbow and hold your hands bit-width apart as though you were holding a tea tray. This image helps you to keep the contact steady. It may help you to imagine you have the bit in your hands. (Photo 1.9)

Above
1.8a and b To get the idea of maintaining the contact and then softening it, practise with a friend holding a rope to represent the reins. If you do not have a handy person, tie the rope to a fence. a) Here we are maintaining a steady contact. Note that my back is hollow and Lorraine's is correct. b) Softening the contact without letting it go loose.

Right
1.9 The hands are close together in a 'normal' position.

- With an unbalanced horse, you may need your hands wider apart than you would on a more advanced horse. A wider contact gives the horse a wider 'passageway' to go along, offering greater stability for the horse's shoulders and helps to prevent wobbles (Photos 1.10a–c). Once the horse becomes more balanced you can return your hands to the tea-tray position and be able to keep your horse straight with just your body, no longer needing the extra support from the reins.

1.10a–c a) Here the hands are held wider apart to help stabilise the horse, with the elbows bent and close to the sides so they are still able to 'roll' to soften the contact.
b) Here the wide hand position is correct but the rider has turned her legs out, which digs the heels into the horse, and tightens the seat muscles.
c) This wide hand position is not correct – the elbows are locked straight with no flexibility, creating a hard contact.

COMMON PROBLEMS

- Simply **slowing down and speeding up is not a half-halt**: the horse can slow down without taking weight behind, consequently, when you ride him forwards again, he speeds up.

- **Sitting crookedly**: a horse cannot halt straight if the rider is not straight. Crookedness can be caused either by the rider leaning to one side with their shoulders, taking the whole upper body to one side, which increases the weight in the saddle on the same side to which the rider is leaning, or by collapsing at the waist, which puts extra weight on the opposite side of the saddle to which the rider is leaning. This puts more weight on one seat bone than the other, making it difficult for the horse to step under behind equally with both hind legs. (Photo 1.11)

- **Uneven rein contact**: having one rein stronger than the other or one hand higher than the other can both cause crookedness in the contact. The horse will tip his ears to one side, so the poll will not be level. This can cause tension in the contact and, if not rectified, can cause physical problems with the poll (summit of occipital crest). The first vertebra, the atlas, forms the atlanto-occipital joint with the occipital bone, which allows the head to nod up and down. The second vertebra, the axis, forms the atlantoaxial joint with the atlas, which allows the head to move from side to side.

- **Elbow and hand position.** Carrying the elbows and hands incorrectly can cause rider position, contact and horse outline problems (Photos 1.12a–k, see overleaf)

- **One stirrup longer than the other** will cause crookedness in the rider, which will transfer to the horse. Check your stirrup length before you get on. Stirrup leathers can stretch and it is usual for the left stirrup leather to become longer as this is the one used all the time if you mount your horse from the left (near) side.

- **Hollowing your back** will tend to make you lean forwards, putting your weight onto the horse's forehand, making it difficult for him to stop. You will then pull your hands back into your stomach. The horse will hollow his back, raise his head, and take the pressure of the bit on his lower jaw – a very unpleasant experience. His reaction will be to run away from this uncomfortable situation.

- **Collapsing into a chair seat** with your weight to the back of the saddle, will push your feet forward in the stirrups, and make you pull back on the reins; this is a sure-fire way to ask the horse to shoot off with you. It is like pressing both feet forwards on the gas pedal. (Photo 1.13)

- **Running a horse into the nearest fence/wall in an effort to stop.** Perhaps this is almost unbelievable but I have witnessed riders doing this! This is a very dangerous thing to do because the horse may be capable of jumping said wall or fence, and so you have to make sure that you are not only capable of the jump as well but also that you know what lies on the other side!

  If you run your horse straight towards a barrier, his alternative action, rather than to jump, may be to turn one way or the other

1.11 leaning to one side creates uneven contact.

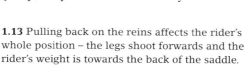

1.13 Pulling back on the reins affects the rider's whole position – the legs shoot forwards and the rider's weight is towards the back of the saddle.

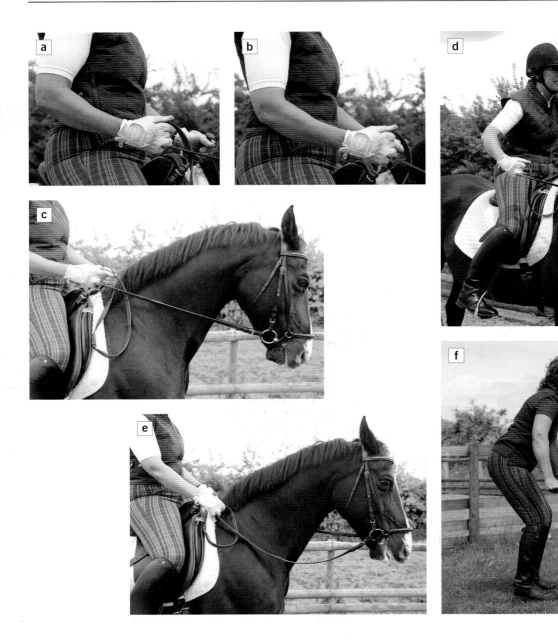

1.12a–k a) Mounted: the elbow has come behind the rider's side seams resulting in a pulling hand. b) Mounted: a correct hand position with a softly closed fist and the elbow by the side. c) Mounted; a correct hand position and correct contact in the halt. d) Mounted: pulling back with the elbows out on the horse. The lower leg is pushed back and the rider's upper body tips forwards. e) Mounted: dropping the contact on the horse. f) On the ground: carrying the hands too low with straight elbows and tense shoulders makes the horse resist the contact. g) Mounted: straight and stiff arms and elbows. h) Mounted: a tense hand causes the horse to resist the contact. i) Mounted: pulling back on the reins with the hands raised and the rider leaning back. j) On the ground: the effect of pulling back on the rider's position. k) On the ground: leaning forwards and dropping the contact makes the horse hollow and may encourage him to run away rather than stop.

when he reaches the wall, and you will have no idea which way the horse may turn. This is a far more likely outcome than him stopping.

In an indoor school, I have also seen riders let their horses run into a corner of the school. This just frightens the horse and will make him paranoid about corners, which can take a very long time to eradicate.

The correct way to use a fence or wall as an optical barrier to help you to stop your horse or to slow down is to ride alongside it on a slight angle, as you would on the last step of a circle. This must be combined with half-halts to steady the horse before then asking for halt.

- Many riders fiddle around with the halt if it is not square. If, for example, your horse does not halt square but leaves a leg out behind, you could try to correct it by using your leg on the same side as the offending leg. If this does not work then you are better off walking forwards and making a new halt with better preparation. If you try to make too many corrections to a halt, your horse will be reluctant to stand still the next time you ask him to stop, so there is a fine balance between making a well-timed aid to correct the horse's balance, and too many taps with the whip, or too many leg aids. If you need to give aids, they should always be given in the rhythm of the horse's gaits. If you are preparing for a halt transition, try counting 1, 2, 3 halt in time with the gait you are in.

RIDDEN EXERCISES

All the following exercises should be ridden on both reins.

Stop Exercise 1

Riding half-halts and halts on a 20m circle On a 20m circle, ride a half-halt as you approach the track on each side of the circle. Add in two more half-halts as you cross the centre line each time, making a total of four half-halts evenly spaced around the circle.

Repeat the exercise using halts instead of half-halts. (Diagram 1)

Stop Exercise 2

Riding a half-halt and halt at each letter around the school You can ride these half-halts in any gait: walk, trot or canter.

Repeat the exercise riding a halt at each letter.

Turn onto the centre line at one end of the school. **Ride several half-halts as you pass down the centre line**, in any gait. (Diagram 2)

Stop Exercise 3

Improving the halt To improve your halt, practise riding several half-halts in walk before riding a halt. Then, ride several half-halts, but walk on again without

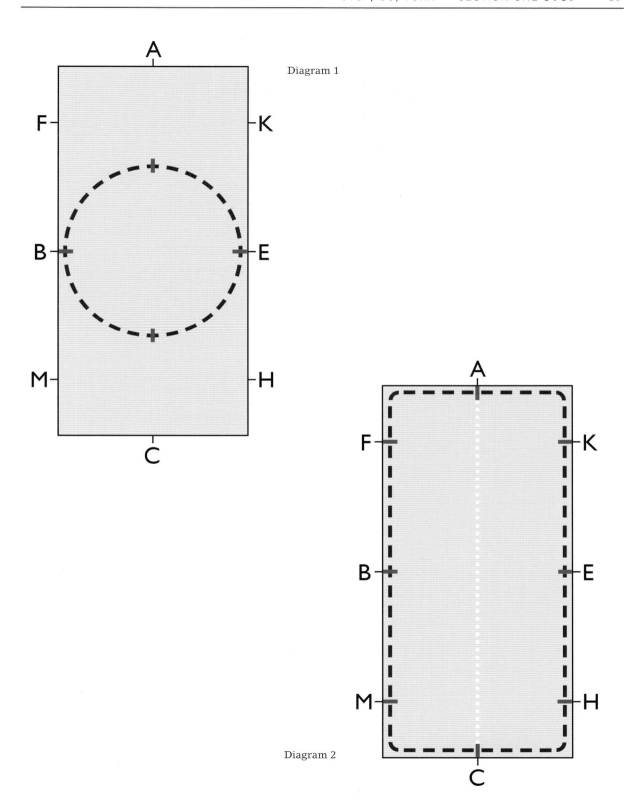

Diagram 1

Diagram 2

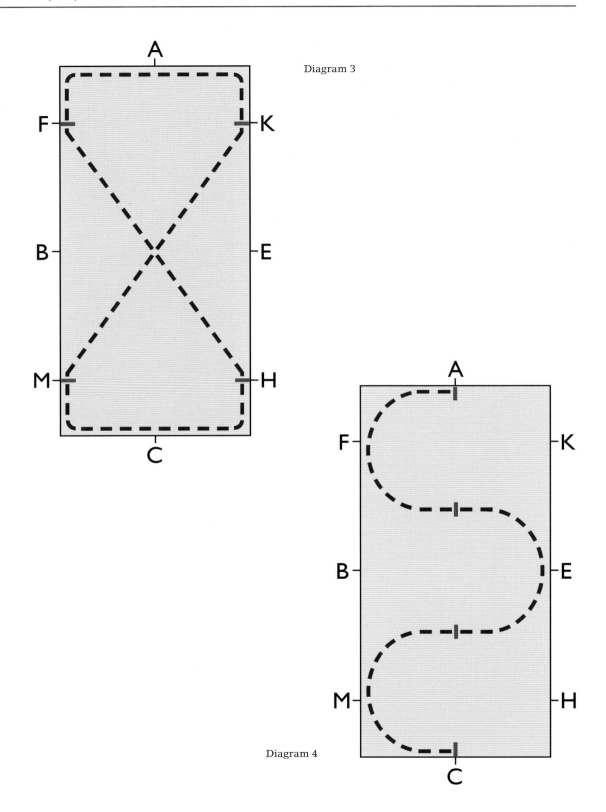

Diagram 3

Diagram 4

actually halting. This helps to keep the horse's weight on his hind legs; to keep energy in the gait – whether in walk, trot or canter – and helps the horse to step well under behind when you do actually halt. By 'rehearsing' the halt in this way with, say, three half-halts before riding the full halt, you should find the horse remains attentive in the halt, with energy, ready to proceed forwards again when you ask him. You do not want a 'dead' halt where your horse has no impetus.

You could ride this on the diagonals of the school, aiming to halt at the end of the diagonal just as you reach the track (Diagram 3).

Stop Exercise 4

Three-loop serpentine Ride a three-loop serpentine halting each time you reach the centre line (see Turn section, page 122, for details on how to ride a serpentine). Repeat the exercise, this time half-halting as you reach the centre line. (Diagram 4)

SECTION TWO
GO

Asking your horse to go should be the easy part because – looking at in the most basic way – as a flight animal the horse wants to flee from danger, so surely all the rider has to do is to stay on!

For a balanced rider who is in tune with her horse both mentally and physically, this should not be a problem. (Photo 2.1) But a horse will refuse to move if he feels uncomfortable, restricted by the rider's position and balance, or if he has no trust in what the rider is asking him to do. For example, a top-class rider can make dramatic cross-country fences look easy but a poor rider puts herself and her horse in mortal danger.

When you want to be 'in motion' with your horse, it is very important that you can co-ordinate your movement with that of your horse, otherwise you are both in for a very uncomfortable ride! It is important to understand how your horse moves: his gaits, the way he moves his limbs and back. Without this understanding, it is impossible for the rider to ride a horse without bouncing around in the saddle. With no connection to the horse's back, it is all too easy to fall off, which is not a pleasant experience for the rider, who may get injured, or the horse.

Riders must be taught the feel of the horse's back from the beginning. Having respect for the living, breathing creature that is allowing you to sit on his back is a very humbling experience.

How does the rider learn how her body influences that of the horse? Many riders tighten their seat muscles in order to push the horse forwards, for example, but this just blocks the horse's back movement. To understand how this feels, practise clenching and relaxing your seat muscles both on and off the horse. (Photos 2.2a and b)

The way to learn to sit on a horse correctly is on the lunge. The lunge is the best way for a skilled instructor with a trained horse to teach a novice rider to understand how a horse moves, thinks and reacts while not having to worry about the control of the horse initially. The sympathetic pupil who really wants to learn will

2.1 Going forwards in balance.

2.2a and b a) Tightening the seat muscles blocks the horse's back movement. (The tightening is illustrated by more creases in the jodhpurs.) b) Relaxed seat muscles allow the rider to move their hips and back with the horse.

soon realise that this is better for her and for the horse. Horses are not machines and neither are they for hauling around and joy riding. In this technological age, there are mechanical horses, computer analysis, and so on, all of which play a role in educating riders, but only by riding the real thing does the rider get a feel for how the horse moves through his back, how he thinks and how he responds to the rider's aids and mental attitude. Asking your horse to go forwards requires a positive mental attitude above all else. Any negative thoughts you have will be picked up by your horse. If you do not believe in him 100 per cent, and he does not believe in you, he will not go large at trot, jump that fence, or go down the centre line of the dressage arena.

There is nothing more enjoyable than developing a true partnership with a horse. Let us think about a scenario so many riders would love to take part in: riding along a beach with the wind blowing in your face. Wouldn't this be far more pleasurable if you knew you were in control, knew that you were not going to fall off and could stop in a moment? It would also be preferable to being carted down the beach by a stiff, unresponsive horse with a back like a plank who just gallops along to the end of the ride and stops because that's what he has been programmed to do; this is not horsemanship.

The Three Basic Gaits

So, how does the horse move? He has three basic gaits: walk, trot and canter.

Walk

The walk is a four-beat gait; each leg moves separately. If the sequence starts with the horse's right hind leg, he then moves his right foreleg, followed by the left hind and finally the left foreleg. So, the walk sequence is right hind, right fore, left hind, left fore, with weight-bearing stages in between (Photos 2.3a–h, see overleaf). His back muscles move in the sequence, left side, right side, corresponding with the leg movements. To go with this movement, the rider's hips should 'walk' with the horse's hips.

Trot

The trot is a two-beat gait; the horse moves his legs in diagonal pairs (Photo 2.4, see overleaf), springing from one pair to the other, creating a moment of suspension where all four feet are off the ground. This is the 'bounce' that you will feel from the saddle. In sitting trot, your hips should 'trot' with the horse as though you were jogging on the ground, with one hip moving forwards and then the other. This corresponds with the horse's hip movement as he steps forwards with each hind leg in turn, at the same time as the opposite front leg. As the horse springs off the ground and 'bounces', you need to allow your lower back and hip joints to act as shock absorbers.

Canter

The canter is a three-beat gait and either the right or left foreleg is the 'leading' leg. If the left hind leg starts the sequence, it is followed by the diagonal pair of the right hind leg and left foreleg coming forward together and then the leading leg,

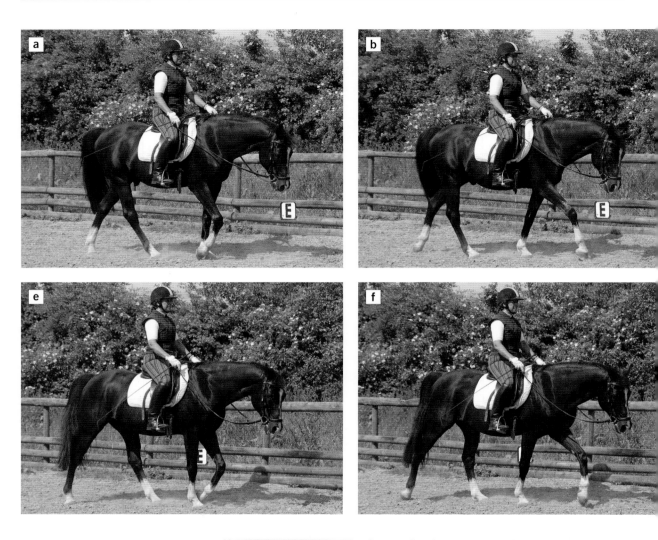

Above and opposite page
2.3a–h Walk sequence: a) The right hind leg steps forwards; b) the right foreleg moves forwards; c) the right foreleg is weight-bearing; d) the left hind leg moves forwards; e) the left hind leg is weight-bearing; f) the left foreleg moves forwards; g) the left foreleg is weight-bearing; h) the right hind leg moves forwards to start the next walk stride sequence.

Right
2.4 The horse's legs move in diagonal pairs in the trot.

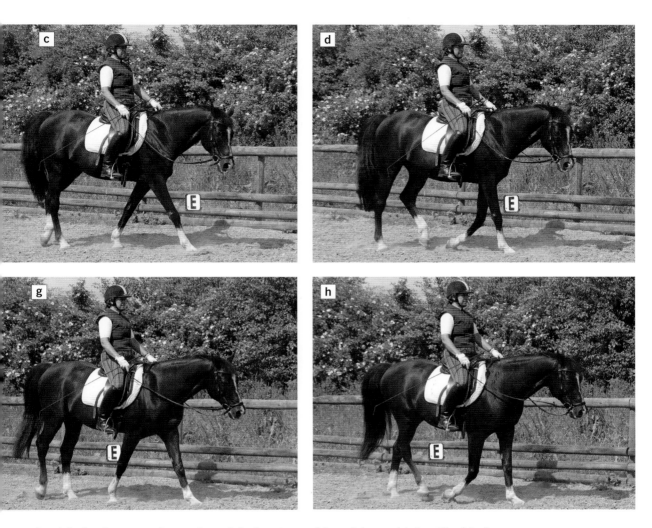

the right foreleg, steps forwards and the horse puts his weight on this leg. The hind legs start to come under to take the weight from the right foreleg. Then all four feet come off the floor in the moment of suspension as the horse tucks its loins in preparation for the next stride. The forehand lifts. The next canter stride starts in the same way from the left hind leg. (Photos 2.5a–f, see overleaf)

It is interesting to note that in the context of riding to music, the canter *could* be described as a four-beat gait, with the moment of suspension as the fourth beat, because you can ride walk and canter to the same four-beat musical track!

Your hips need to 'canter' with the horse. In right-lead canter, your left outside leg gives the first aid, and your left hip moves forwards with the left hind leg as it takes the first step. Then your right hip moves forwards with the horse's right hind leg as this leg and the left foreleg move forwards together and stays forwards as he steps forwards with his right leading leg. As the horse springs off the ground in the moment of suspension, you must lift his back with your back and thighs together,

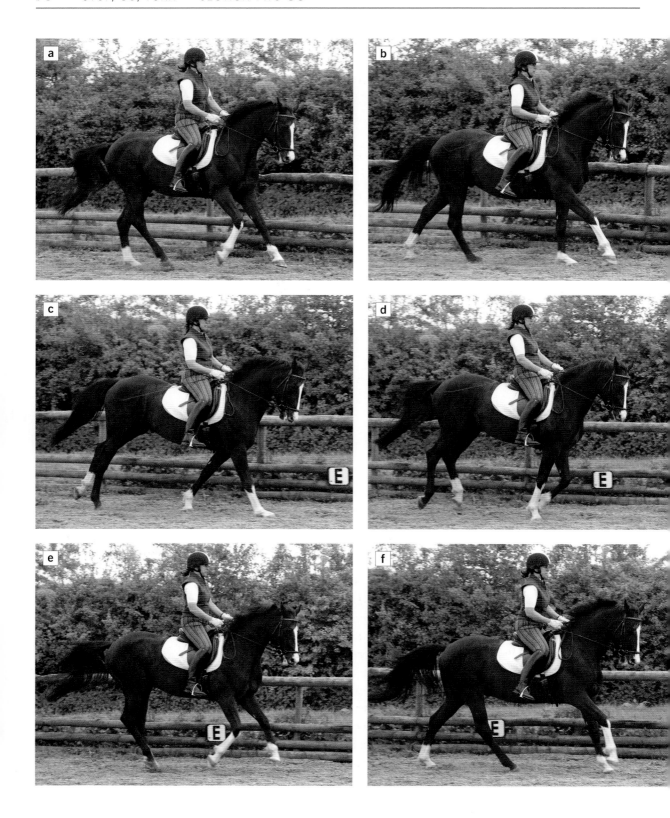

allowing him to tuck his loins in readiness for the next step. Reverse these aids for left-lead canter.

The rider's good position and aids will ensure the horse performs a good canter in a good outline (Photo 2.6).

Asking your Horse to Move

Most riders will use their legs to ask the horse to move forwards. But there are many versions of leg use, some correct and some wrong. The latter is often represented by people tensing their backsides, and jabbing the horse in his sides with their heels. The poor horse reacts sharply, either by shooting forwards, or he may buck or rear if he really takes exception to this 'aid'.

To ask your horse to go, squeeze the horse with both legs at the same time with the top half of your calves. Maintain a light contact with your knees and thighs to keep the horse straight and to control the speed at which you wish to go. Just squeezing with your legs will say, 'Go', but you also need to tell the horse at what speed you wish to go and in which gait. This is where your hips and back come into it.

2.6 In this canter, the rider's inside leg is too far back and she is leaning forwards, causing the horse to raise his neck. If her inside leg was in the correct place by the girth, he would be in a better, more rounded outline. The inside leg helps to keep the horse into the rein contact.

Walk

Walking from halt

Let's start with walking on from a halt on a loose rein. Make sure your position is correct. Squeeze with both calves and, as you feel your horse begin to move, allow your hips to move with his back muscles, so you are allowing him to move forwards. Repeat the squeeze rhythmically with the walk. Some instructors will tell you to use alternate legs as you feel the horse's belly swing right and left as he brings each hind leg forwards in turn. If you get the timing wrong, however, this disturbs the rhythm of the walk, and the horse can pace, i.e. walk like a camel with both legs on the same side moving together, causing a two-beat gait instead of a four-beat gait. It can also cause the horse to waddle from side to side instead of striding straight forwards under his body. Keep your upper body still and your core muscles tight; all you need to do is to move with your lower back and hips. Look forwards between the horse's ears and believe that he will listen to you.

Once your horse is walking, keep going for a few minutes to allow him to relax into a steady rhythm and then take up your rein contact. As you do this, use half-halts to ask him to step under behind so he remains balanced as you bring him into the rein contact with your back and legs. You are, therefore, effectively walking

Opposite page
2.5a–f a) The canter strike-off with the left hind leg. b) The right diagonal pair of legs stepping forwards, namely the right hind leg and left foreleg together. c) The right leading leg steps forwards and takes the weight. d) The hind legs start to come under the body to take the weight from the right foreleg. e) All four feet come off the ground – the moment of suspension – as the horse tucks his loins in preparation for the next stride. f) The next canter stride starts in the same way.

with him as you 'squash' him together so that he lifts his back and arches his neck forwards to the bit. Now you are walking 'on the bit' or 'in a rounded outline', whichever expression you prefer (Photo 2.7).

Use half-halts at frequent intervals to maintain this outline and use them *before* you lose the outline and balance; this is far easier than not being aware of your horse losing his balance. If he does lose his balance, you will need to halt and start again with a new walk transition.

If the walk becomes hurried, use half-halts to steady it. If it becomes too slow, then you will need to squeeze more firmly, but in the rhythm of the walk. To speed up the walk, use your back and walk quicker with your hips, the horse will walk quicker with you. If your seat is tight, this will render your leg aids ineffective. So check that your hip and leg aids are working in unison. If this does not work, a short sharp tap with a schooling whip by your calf may be necessary.

Think of a whip as a third leg and you will not go wrong with its application. It is an aid, not a punishment. The whip must back-up a leg aid in an instant. There is no point just whacking the horse randomly. You must make it clear to him what you are asking from your back and legs first.

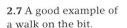

2.7 A good example of a walk on the bit.

Trot

Transition from walk to trot

Once you are in walk, the next thing to do is to ride a transition from walk to trot. Many riders grip the reins tightly in preparation for this because they are worried about losing control of the horse once he starts to trot. Of course, this just makes the horse anxious and tense, which frightens the rider even more. A tense rider usually crouches forwards, losing their core stability, and takes their lower legs away from the horse's sides, being afraid the horse will go too fast if they keep their legs on.

The basic rule is: only ask for what you can control, both mentally and physically. If you are out for a ride with friends and they all want to go for a jolly around the field, and all you want to do is to have a calm walk around, you will not be in the right frame of mind for a speedy canter. Herd instinct will ensure your horse wants to go with his pals, so you will be on a hiding to nothing and will be going for that canter regardless of what you actually want to do. It is always important, therefore, to choose your hacking partner/s wisely!

If your horse does not respond to light aids and you need a firm rein contact for him to take any notice of you, you must have a firm position to match. Your rein contact should never be firmer than your back and legs. Keep your shoulders back and down to maintain your arm and upper body position, and maintain firm core muscles as well; this is your half-halt aid. Once your horse has softened to your aids, then you can soften your muscle tone. Your horse will let you know what you need to do to steady him in his gait – just listen to him!

So, to ask your horse to trot, maintain a steady rein contact which, hopefully, you will have already sorted out in the walk. The horse should be quietly chewing the bit. Squeeze with both calves, asking the horse to go. As you feel him step into trot, trot with your hips. This motion helps the horse to bring each hind foot forwards under his body. If he is stepping forwards correctly, each hind foot should step into the print of the front foot on the same side; this is known as tracking up (Photo 2.8).

2.8 A good example of a balanced, active trot. The right hind foot steps into the print of the right fore foot; this is known as tracking up.

Keep sufficient contact with your thighs and knees to keep your balance and to ask the horse to go in a straight line. Maintain an even contact with both reins as he steps into trot.

You will need to use your upper body to stabilise your hand position by keeping your tummy muscles firm, and carrying your hands in the tea-tray position.

Sitting trot

For sitting trot, trot with your hips and, as your seat remains in contact with the saddle, allow the muscles and joints of your seat, back and legs to absorb the spring as the horse jumps from one diagonal pair to the other.

To bring the trot down to the walk, brace your back and half-halt a few times to steady, collect, the trot before coming back into walk mode with your hips. The horse should walk with you. If he does not, do the same aid again more firmly, closing your thighs and knees sufficiently to block the trot.

Rising trot

With rising trot you lift your weight out of the saddle on one beat of the trot and sit on the next. It is an action that takes the pressure off the horse's back muscles. In rising trot, it is usual to sit in the saddle as the horse's inside hind leg and outside foreleg are on the ground. As you do this, the outside hind leg and inside foreleg swing forwards. A stiff horse that may be reluctant to step under behind on a circle may benefit by being ridden on the other diagonal, with the rider sitting as the outside hind leg is in contact with the ground, which prevents the horse escaping with his haunches to the outside, and frees up the inside hind leg, enabling it to swing forwards easily. In my opinion, the horse benefits from the rider being able to ride all school movements changing diagonal frequently.

Many riders are taught to rise to the trot before learning to sit to the trot. I think this is a mistake because, unless the rider can sit to the trot and under-stand how the horse moves his back and legs in the trot, and how to maintain a steady contact, the rising trot can be very unbalancing for the horse. Often a rider moves her hands up and down with her body, which gives the poor horse a jerk in the mouth at every step. The horse then raises his neck and hollows his back to avoid this.

You need a secure lower leg and knee position to ride a good rising trot. Keep your weight on the balls of your feet, and lower your heels, keeping your ankles flexible and your toes relaxed. Gripping the stirrups with your toes will make you feel like a parrot on a perch!

To rise, raise your hips up and towards the horse's withers, leaning a little forward as you do so. This will enable you to keep your balance as the horse moves forwards in trot. (Photos 2.9a–c) If you stand straight up, you will fall backwards,

2.9a–c a) Sitting in the saddle as the outside hind leg and inside foreleg leave the ground, and the inside hind leg and outside foreleg are on the ground. b) Starting to rise out of the saddle as the outside hind leg and inside foreleg are coming onto the ground. c) Rising fully out of the saddle as the horse is about to spring onto the other diagonal pair.

and you will get left behind the horse's movement. Straighten your knees, but do not lock them straight; they should be slightly bent to retain their flexibility.

Once you are up, lower yourself smoothly back into the saddle again. Keep your thighs firm as this will prevent you banging down into the saddle; your seat's contact with the saddle should be only light so that you are ready to rise again at the next step.

To come back to the walk from rising trot, close your lower legs and knees to steady the trot. As the trot collects, feel the moment the horse wants to come back into a walk, and sit at exactly that moment. This avoids the bumping around in the saddle that can be the risk if you try to come back into a sitting trot to steady the horse. Unless you have steadied the trot first, sitting trot will be ungainly.

Canter

Canter aids

Once you are going along merrily in sitting trot with your hips moving with the horse's back, we can come to the canter aid.

If you wish to canter left, the 'outside' will be on the right and the 'inside' on the left of you and your horse. For canter right, this is reversed. (See the Turn section on page 106 for a full explanation of the inside and outside aids.)

To initiate the canter left, turn your hips a little to the left. Your first leg aid should be with your outside leg placed behind the girth, asking the outside hind to start the canter sequence. Next, put a little weight on your outside seat bone to ensure the outside hind leg steps forwards and not out to the side.

Then press your inside hip forwards as the horse's inside hind leg moves forwards. Move this hip forwards again, i.e. a double beat, as he steps forwards with his leading (left) leg. Next, close both legs, and lift him 'up off the ground' with your thighs. Repeat this every stride.

Transition from canter to trot

To ride a downward transition from canter to trot, reposition your outside leg so that it is parallel with your inside leg. Use a half-halt at each stride to collect the canter and trot with your hips so you come out of the canter rhythm (three beats, with a moment of suspension) into the two-beat trot rhythm. Three to five half-halts should be enough.

It is important to collect, or steady, the canter before asking for trot to avoid crashing onto the horse's back. If you miss the moment to give you a smooth transition, then go into rising trot.

Maintenance of contact and position in gait transitions

It is important to ride forwards into, and maintain, a steady contact with the reins as you make transitions between the gaits (Photo 2.10). You need to keep a constant position with your upper body in order to do this. Your arm joints, namely the shoulder, elbow, wrist and fingers all have a role to play when trying to keep a steady contact. Think of keeping the bit still, rather than keeping your hands still; trying to keep your hands still in relation to your body results in your hands moving about. Keep the bit still by using your arms as shock absorbers to do so. To get a feel for this, try walking along carrying a cup of tea, and notice how you have to use your arm to avoid spilling it.

Remember, however, that a steady contact should never mean that you hold on to the reins in order to support your balance (Photo 2.11).

In walk, your body should move in a subtle manner to allow the horse to use his whole back and neck as he moves. The bigger the walk stride, the more the horse will need to move his neck, but he should not be wiggling his head about; it should be still, and you should maintain a steady contact with the bit. Your arms should absorb the movement of the horse's neck: they should not be used in an excessive rowing motion pushing backwards and forwards, nor should your hands move around or fiddle with the bit.

In trot, there will be a slight shimmy of your shoulders as the horse moves. This is a ripple effect flowing up from your hips and lower back as they move with the horse's back, and this movement filters up through the rest of your spine, diminishing as it goes. If this is achieved you will look and feel at one with your horse. Many riders nod their heads in trot, thinking this gives them a supple back, but the opposite is true. A rider with a supple back will keep the head still, in the same way that a supple horse will keep his head and neck still in the trot. It is important that the hands remain still, and do not move right-left-right-left with your hips.

In canter, your hands must remain still, to keep the bit steady and level in the horse's mouth. Your elbows act as the link between your back movement and the steadiness of the horse's head. Aim to keep the bit steady and level in the horse's mouth. Your elbows should move subtly by your sides, each elbow moving slightly forwards with the hip on the same side to correspond to the horse's movement.

Above left
2.10 Riding forwards into a steady contact with the horse in a correct outline.

Above right
2.11 Being able to soften the rein contact is a test of good balance.

Understanding Rhythm and Tempo

Rhythm is a regular sequence of beats. Tempo is the speed of the rhythm. Each of the horse's gaits has a rhythm. Going faster or slower in the gaits affects the tempo by increasing or decreasing it.

Rhythm

Rhythm is the beat of the gait: the horse's walk has a four-beat rhythm, the trot has a two-beat rhythm, and the canter has three beats (plus a moment of suspension between each stride when all four feet are off the ground). Every stride in each gait should be in the same rhythm, i.e. the beats as the hooves hit the ground should be in a regular sequence. This, in horsey terms, is described as 'regularity'.

If a horse does not have regularity, he has either a physical problem or is tense. Pain will affect regularity, so the horse who moves irregularly may be lame. Tension, whatever the cause, affects the whole horse, one symptom of which is irregular steps. Tension can be caused by the rider either holding the contact too tightly, being tense in their back or seat muscles, or giving aids at the wrong moment. It is most important that any aids the rider gives the horse are in the rhythm of the gait. Mistimed aids will disturb the rhythm and affect the regularity of the horse's strides.

If you are competing in dressage, you will lose marks if your horse has an irregular gait.

From a physical point of view, if your horse cannot or will not work in rhythm, in one or all of his gaits, this must be rectified. Long-term irregularity will affect the horse's muscular development, and he will become crooked.

If he has pain in one leg and the rider does not notice, but tries to work the horse regardless, the horse will compensate for his discomfort in various ways. He may take a shorter step with his painful leg, which over time becomes weak; this will have a knock-on effect on the horse's back muscles. The rider may notice that they are sitting to one side of the saddle. This may be due to the horse pushing the rider's weight to one side so he can carry the weight on his good leg. Quite often, riders will attempt to fix this issue by getting their saddle checked by the saddler, or by buying a dynamic saddle pad, but omit to check their horse's muscular development carefully, which will give clues as to the problem.

Some riders will ignore the signs of discomfort from their horse and kick on attempting to ride their horse more forwards to improve the rhythm but all they are doing is asking the horse to run on his forehand.

If the problem is with a hind leg, the horse may hollow his back and trail his hind legs out behind, which results in the weight not being taken correctly behind, and the muscles of the haunches not working properly, thus they become weak.

If the problem is with a front leg, the rider may detect this by having issues with, for example, extending the trot, when the horse has to move more through the shoulder and spring more from all four feet. To avoid putting extra pressure on his painful front foot, the horse will tend to run faster, tensing his back and scurrying along the ground to avoid the additional concussion. And so, what started with lameness on one leg ends up as a back problem for the horse as well. The owner then gets carried away with veterinary treatment, chiropractors, and other practitioners, without looking for the simple solution first, which is to check your own position in the saddle to make sure you are sitting straight and evenly weighted on both seat bones.

The simplest explanation for a horse being irregular could be a small stone in the hoof, so this is always worth checking for first!

Tempo

Tempo is the speed of the rhythm. For example, if you are in a rhythmic four-beat walk, you could walk faster or slower. The 1,2,3,4 of the steps can be speeded up or slowed down. This is not the same as collecting and extending. You can ride a slow collected walk, and a fast collected walk, or a slow extended trot, and a faster one.

Forwardness explained – power not speed!

Another common expression is 'forwardness', which does not mean going faster and faster. It is attitude rather than speed; a horse can be forwards thinking in halt!

Your horse must be willing and listening to what you are asking him to do. You achieve this by preparing your horse with half-halts so that he is balanced and able to respond to your aids for the next movement, transition etc.

A lazy or reluctant horse does not go because he is not thinking forwards. He may have tightness in his back, a saddle that does not fit or, most commonly, a rider who is blocking his forwards motion with a tight seat. Forcing him by kicking will not be the answer. Improve your seat, and your horse will go!

A forward horse is responsive and light to your aids. If you can stop your horse easily, he is balanced enough to go forwards in control.

In order to go forwards, your horse needs impulsion, or controlled energy. Increasing energy, or asking for more impulsion does not require an increase in the miles per hour you are travelling at. Collected movements such as piaffe, where the horse moves in a trot sequence on the spot, requires a huge amount of impulsion, much more than a horse tearing along on his forehand in a bad example of an extended trot.

Collecting and extending v. speeding up and slowing down

Collection

Collection is riding a smaller stride while maintaining the same rhythm and tempo. To collect the horse, use half-halts and transitions to balance the horse on his haunches, taking weight behind. Brace your back and close your legs to hold the horse more on the spot, shortening his steps. Do a smaller walking motion with your hips to match the horse's back movement. This aid is the same for walk, trot and canter. As the haunches lower, the forehand raises, and the horse arches his neck more, appearing rounder and more squashed together or shorter in his outline. Collection prepares the horse for extension, a bit like changing gear downwards, to increase the traction with the hind legs. Without collecting the horse to prepare him, he will not go forwards in a correct extension, but run along on his forehand out of balance.

Extension

Extension is riding a bigger stride while maintaining the same rhythm and tempo. From collection, move more with your back and hips to make a bigger stride, whether in walk, trot or canter. (Photo 2.12) The horse will need to arch his neck more forwards as he uses the impulsion, generated from collecting him in the first

2.12 A good example of extending the stride in canter.

place, to push more from behind so you must allow him to do this by softening the reins and not hanging onto the bit. This action would restrict the length of his strides, causing him to potter along with quick, short steps. Too strong a contact will prevent him from extending through his shoulders and not allow him to step forwards under his body with his hind legs. (Photos 2.13a–c)

2.13a–c a) Riding forwards correctly in trot with the horse in a rounded outline with the poll the highest point. b) Too much rein contact causes resistance and blocks the hind legs from stepping under. c) A good length of stride when extending, but the contact could be softer allowing the neck to reach forwards.

Speeding up

Speeding up is maintaining collection or extension and the rhythm, but increasing the tempo. For example, if the collected walk is too slow it becomes a shuffle and the back feet may not take the same length of stride as the front feet. Speeding it up a bit will improve the activity of the steps, with the horse picking his feet up rather than dragging his toes in the sand.

Slowing down

Slowing down is maintaining collection or extension and the rhythm, but decreasing the tempo. If your collected walk is too fast, your horse may jog instead, or lean against the contact for support hollowing his back as he finds it difficult to maintain rhythm in the speed of walk you are asking for. Slowing it down will relax the horse and enable him to work in a better outline and balance.

The correct speed for the horse is one where he is able to work in balance, in a correct outline, and in rhythm. He will feel easy to ride.

Rider Posture and its Influence on the Aids to Go

How to move in good posture

The importance of walking

In order to move with your horse, your joints must be flexible and one of the best exercises to achieve this flexibility is simply to walk but *how* you walk is important.

There is no point in slouching along, shuffling your feet; you should stand tall, stretching up through your spine with your hips upright. Keep your shoulders back and down, your head straight with your arms by your sides. Sounds familiar? Yes – this is exactly the same body position you should have when riding!

You can walk anywhere and at any time: when you are leading your horse to the field, walking the dog or going shopping. If you are lucky enough to have some time on your hands, put on your walking boots and head for the hills! Hill work is not just for getting horses fit – it works for riders too!

When you are walking, be aware of how your hips move alternately as you take each step. Feel how your lumbar muscles (the 'jeans back-pockets' muscles) and your abdominal muscles work as you move. Make sure you take the same length of step with each leg. If you take a shorter step with one leg, this can indicate that you are tighter on one side of your body than the other. This will have a knock-on effect on your horse; if you are unable to walk with regular steps you can hardly expect your horse to do so!

Walk briskly and swing your arms with each stride. Breathe deeply and be aware of your surroundings. By all means pay attention to where you are putting your feet, but try not to stare at the ground all the time!

Use all your senses. Focus your sight not only directly in front of you, but also be aware of your peripheral vision, everything that you can see around you. Listen to the sounds you hear: the birds singing, the wind rustling through the trees, or the traffic thundering past. What can you smell: the blossom on the trees, fresh-baked bread from the bakery, or traffic fumes?

Try to get used to using your sight, hearing and sense of smell to enhance your general awareness. It may sound a bit silly, but you will need to do the same when you ride, not only from a safety point of view, but also from a relaxation aspect when riding your horse. Being a flight animal, your horse is on red alert at all times, so you need to be aware of things that might affect him, without being paranoid, so that you can take the role of herd leader and reassure him and hold his hand, or rather hoof, to show him the world is OK.

As you walk, be aware of how your hip, knee and ankle joints bend and straighten with each step. Use your feet properly from heel to toe. 'Peel' your feet off the ground with each step and place them smoothly on the ground again rather than thump them down on the ground. Your joints act as shock absorbers. Use them to cushion each step and avoid concussion. Jarring steps will not do any part of your body any good and most likely give you backache.

Be aware when you walk of the rise and fall of each stride as you transfer your weight from one leg to the other. This mimics the horse's back movement. His back moves the same way as yours. Each side of his back moves as he steps forwards with each hind leg in turn; when you are in the saddle you will feel a lift as he picks each foot up. By moving exactly with the horse's back – in the same way as you walk on the ground – you will allow the horse's back to move underneath you when you are in the saddle.

2.14 Sitting level and in a good position helps the horse to remain in balance when he is going forwards.

How to support the horse without blocking his back movement

To avoid blocking your horse's back movement, you must be balanced. Leaning one way or the other will block one side of the horse's back by overloading it. Your upper body position plays a very important role in this. (Photo 2.14)

Think of your upper body as being divided into three parts.

1. The top part: your shoulder area.

2. The middle part: your core muscles (stomach and back).

3. The lower part: your hips (pelvis).

These three parts must be stacked in alignment, one on top of the other like building blocks, for you to be in balance. Leaning to one side or twisting either your shoulders or your hips disturbs this alignment, putting you out of balance. Only a balanced rider achieves balance with the horse. If you are balanced, your horse can move easily with you on board.

You need to maintain good core strength to retain this posture while moving with your horse. Many riders try too hard to relax when they ride, so they flop around in the saddle and flopping has nothing to do with relaxation. Relaxation is a state of mind in this instance; a relaxed rider has good muscle tone and is able to move in harmony with the horse.

If moving exactly in tune with a horse, a rider will appear to be sitting still, whereas they are in fact moving continually but moving the right parts at the right time. A good illustration of this is to compare a couple of professional ballroom dancers with a less experienced couple. The first couple are a pleasure to watch, flowing effortlessly and as one around the dance floor, but the second couple are forever stepping on each others' toes and dragging each other around the floor!

Suppling exercises

Hips

One of the best and easiest ways to loosen your hips and to get them moving is to walk (see page 16).

Another useful hip loosener is to circle your hips each way (see page 23).

- When you are suitably supple, you will find that to collect the horse in any gait, all you need to do is simply make a smaller movement with your hips, thus reducing the length of the horse's strides. But remember that collected steps must have more lift, i.e. what they lose in length, they gain in height. This maintains the energy in the gait. To extend the steps, do a bigger hip movement, allowing the horse to move more freely. You should maintain a correct upper body position with your core muscles tight while moving your hips.

Spine

A good exercise to relax your spine is to curl it down.

- Start by bending the knees, tuck your pelvis under then, lowering your chin towards your chest, begin to roll down through the spine while keeping the shoulders, arms and neck completely relaxed but the tummy muscles tight. If your back is stiff, you may only get as far as your knees at first, but gently and slowly repetition of this exercise will help you to loosen up. When you have curled down as far as you can, uncurl your spine slowly, straightening your knees and hips first, and finishing with your shoulders and head. It is important to do this exercise with your knees bent to make sure your whole spine bends. (Photos 2.15a–d)

2.15a–d a) Lower your chin to your chest, round your shoulders and bend the knees, curling forwards keeping your tummy tight. b) Lower your upper body curling your spine with your hands at just below knee height. You may only get this far if your back is tight. Then lower your body, fold from the hips and bend your knees more to touch the ground with your hands. c) Slowly unroll to halfway. d) Gradually uncurl the top of your spine.

Understanding the rider's hip movement in walk and trot

Try 'walking' and 'trotting' with your hips to some music as you stand on the spot. Keep to the correct rhythm and practise making bigger and smaller movements, as though collecting and extending your horse's strides.

Stand in riding position with your knees slightly bent. Put your fingers on your hip bones and make the walking motion with your hips. Feel your hips moving forwards on one side and then the other; this is the same movement as you need in the saddle to move with the horse's back.

Now try the same thing in a trot motion, moving your hips forward alternately. In between the right/left movement, straighten your knees a little and stand taller to give you the 'up' phase of the trot: the moment when the horse springs from one diagonal to the other (the phase of suspension).

Understanding the rider's hip movement in canter

Stand in riding position with your feet parallel. To move your hips as though asking for left lead canter, firstly place more weight on your right foot; this will be your outside leg. Now transfer your weight to your left foot: your inside leg. As you do this, push your left hip forwards over your left knee. Come back to the centre with your weight on both feet, and stand tall. Repeat this hip movement at every stride. This flowing movement mimics the horse's stride in canter – starting with his outside hind, then the inside diagonal pair, then the left leading leg. Finally comes the moment of suspension.

For right lead canter, do the same movement in mirror image, starting with your weight on your outside foot (the left) transferring it to your inside foot (your right), not forgetting the 'lift' for the moment of suspension.

Once you have the feeling of a single stride each way, try making several in succession, so you get the feeling of the canter rhythm – 1, 2, 3, up. If you are not self-conscious, cantering around the garden on your own two feet is a valuable exercise – you may want to do this after dark when the neighbours have drawn their curtains! Or get the children playing horses and then you can join in!

If you are proficient at this, try building up to some flying changes, where you spring, or hop, from one canter lead to the other, changing the canter lead every 4, 3, 2, strides, or even at every stride for one-time changes!

COMMON PROBLEMS

- **Asking for too much speed makes the horse tense and unbalanced**. His steps will be short and fast. Going too fast in the walk will usually result in the horse jogging, or breaking into trot because he finds it difficult to maintain the walk rhythm at the speed you are asking for. Your horse may break the rhythm of the walk and start to pace, which is when the walk has a two-time beat instead of a four-time beat because both legs on one side move together, followed by both legs on the other side; a camel walks in this way.

   If you trot too fast, your horse may break into a canter because he cannot maintain the trot rhythm at the speed you are asking for. The trot may become four-time with the legs moving individually rather than in individual pairs. This gait is known as the tölt and is the fifth gait for Icelandic ponies, who are famous for this gait. Going too fast in canter does not really need any explanation – you will be out of control! Stopping and turning will be difficult at the very least!

- **Going too slowly** makes it difficult for the horse to step under behind to generate impulsion. The horse may find it difficult to sustain any gait in this case.

- **Not giving aids in the rhythm of the gait**. Your aids are most effective if given in time with the horse's movement. With a correct contact with your seat, you can synchronise your back and hip movements with your horse's back movement, which should be comfortable for both horse and rider. If you have no coordination, you will bump around on your horse's back. He will tense his back and neck, and tighten his mouth against the rein contact in an effort to let you know you are not getting things right.

- **Unsteady contact.** Not maintaining a steady contact at all times disturbs the rhythm and balance. If the horse is wiggling his nose from side to side because of this, it will be difficult to keep him straight.

- **Holding the reins too tightly.** Hanging onto the contact too tightly will prevent your horse from going forwards from your leg aids. (Photos 2.16a–d, see overleaf)

- **Moving the shoulders instead of the hips** will affect the horse's balance. If the arms and hands move as well, then the contact is also affected. Many riders have difficulty distinguishing one part of their body from the other! If a rider has stiff hip joints, they may move their shoulders instead in an effort to go with the horse. This excessive shoulder movement manifests itself either by tipping the shoulders from side to side, or rotating them, or by rocking the upper body forwards and backwards. Tensing the shoulders will block the horse's forwards

2.16a–d a) On the ground: holding tightly with the elbows locked straight inhibits forwards movement. b) On the horse: Holding tightly with the elbows locked straight. c) On the ground: pulling back with the elbows out also causes resistance to the contact from the horse. d) On the horse: pulling back with the elbows out.

motion and the rider usually ends up kicking like mad to counter this! (Photos 2.17a and b)

- **Tension in the rider's neck and jaw** will transfer to the horse via the rein contact. It is quite surprising how the horse mirrors, so a relaxed happy rider will have a relaxed happy horse. (Photo 2.18)

2.17a and b a) Tense shoulders restrict forward motion. b) Relaxed shoulders allow the horse to go forwards in balance

2.18 A happy horse with a soft, steady contact and a relaxed jaw, softly mouthing the bit.

- **Losing core strength**, i.e. collapsing the core muscles and moving too much in the saddle, is very common. It is usually a result of the rider overdoing it in their effort to move with the horse. The remedy is to sit stiller and taller. (Photo 2.19)

- **Moving the hips together, i.e. pushing with the seat**, instead of moving them alternately right/left with the horse's back. Many riders are not aware that the horse's back moves in two halves. Pushing with both seat bones together blocks the horse's natural back movement, making it impossible for the horse to sustain his rhythm and energy (impulsion).

- **Moving the hips in a rolling motion from side to side**. This is common in canter, with riders doing a circular hula-hula dance movement with their hips instead of a cantering movement. Rolling around in the saddle causes the horse to roll in his canter, which affects his balance, making it impossible for him to canter in 'four-wheel drive' with his hind legs taking weight.

2.19 Collapsing the core muscles results in a lack of body control, and the rider tries to hold the reins too strongly to compensate.

RIDDEN EXERCISES

All the following exercises should be ridden on both reins.

Go Exercise 1

Rising trot exercise In rising trot, go large around the school on the track and rise up and down on alternate strides, then stand up for two strides, sit for two; stand up for three strides, sit for three; stand up for four strides, sit for four; and so on. (Diagram 5)

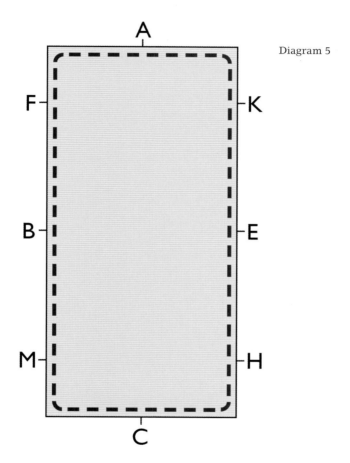

Diagram 5

Go Exercise 2

Changing gear on a circle On a 20m circle, change gear in each gait from collected walk to medium walk and from medium walk to extended walk before going back down through the gears to collected walk. You can put in as many gears as you like; for example, first gear being extreme collected walk, and tenth gear

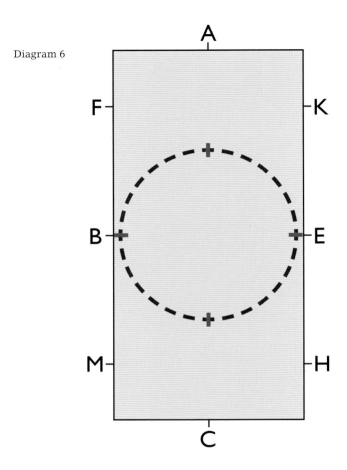

Diagram 6

being the biggest extended walk you can achieve. Aim to change gear each quarter of the circle. (Diagram 6)

Go Exercise 3

Speeding up and slowing down Practise speeding up and slowing down in each gait without losing rhythm and balance. Ride around the school on the inside track, making sure you keep your horse straight. (Diagram 7) Ride a few steps in a medium walk; slow it down, then speed up again. It must still retain the qualities of a medium walk. Ride the same exercise in trot. Begin with working trot, slow it down, then speed it up. The length of stride and outline must not alter – just the speed – increasing and decreasing the tempo.

Go Exercise 4

Transitions Ride transitions between walk and trot, trot and canter. Practise going from a collected walk to a collected trot, and to a collected canter.

Go around the whole school, with a transition to a new gait at the middle of each side. (Diagram 8)

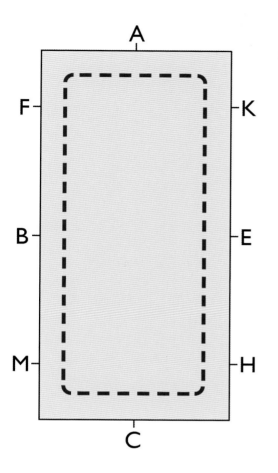

Diagram 7

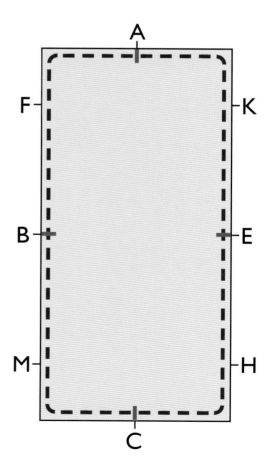

Diagram 8

TURN

The Importance of the Turn

When riding our horses, it is impossible to participate in any activities without being able to turn at some point.

If you are hacking out, you may need to avoid a tree or bush in your path and on the road you will need to turn corners at road junctions.

With show jumping and cross-country, you need to be able to make accurate turns towards the obstacles to present your horse with an accurate approach. Jumping from an acute angle will result in him refusing or running out at the fence, as he will be unable to take off from both hind legs together, i.e. he will not be straight. So, being able to turn your horse makes it easy to come to each fence straight on.

In dressage and everyday schooling, you will not make it around the school or dressage arena without being able to turn.

Being able to turn your horse requires two elements – firstly he must flex at the poll, just behind the ears, so he can look where he is going. Next, he must bend through his body from his head to his tail. From this starting point of flexion and bend, you can progress to riding turns, circles, and lateral movements, (going sideways) which are a necessary part of schooling your horse to maintain and improve his suppleness. (Photo 3.1)

The terms 'turn' and 'corner' mean the same thing and instructors might use either, but I have used 'turn' throughout this section to avoid confusion.

3.1 Turning to the rider's right, showing good flexion and bend but the haunches are in slightly.

Flexion and Bend and the Difference between the Two

Flexion

Flexion is the movement of the horse's head which occurs at the poll joint, just behind the horse's ears. If you feel his neck immediately behind the base of his ears, you will feel two bumps. These are the edge of his skull. The skull connects to the first vertebra of the spine, the atlas, forming the atlanto-occipital joint. From this point the horse can flex his poll vertically, i.e. he can nod his head up and down. The second vertebra is the axis, which forms the atlantoaxial joint with the atlas. It is from this point that the horse is able to turn his head from side to side.

You can feel these movements for yourself. Place one hand on the horse's nose bone and the other on his cheek to keep his head straight, and to reassure him in case he wonders what you are doing! Gently press on his nose bone, and release the pressure again. You should see his head flex downwards and up again to the starting position. Only do this lightly – there is no need to move his head dramatically!

Now try lateral, i.e. side to side, flexion. Stand to one side of the horse and place one hand on his cheek and the other on his nose as before. This time, gently draw his head towards you, and release, using the hand on his cheek to prevent any twisting. He should turn his head slightly towards you. Stand on the other side of the horse, and try from this direction. Again, the horse should turn his head slightly towards you. (Photos 3.2a and b)

3.2a and b Flexing the horse's head at the poll from the saddle.
a) Flexion to the rider's right. b) Flexion to the rider's left.

If your horse has any stiffness at the poll, this is a good way of finding out. You may find he can flex one way more easily than the other, or may be reluctant to nod his head. If he reacts sharply to vertical or lateral flexion, he may have pain or discomfort in the poll area, of may be very stiff. If he has not been ridden properly on the bit, not allowed to stretch and never learnt to relax into the rein contact, then this is likely.

Stiffness in the poll is common with horses who have been ridden in gadgets such as draw reins, which give a false roundness with the horse being over-bent, looking back at his knees. Unfortunately these days, many riders ride their horses in this position, i.e. behind the vertical, thinking that this indicates the horse is on the bit. For a horse to be properly flexed at the poll his head should be vertical to the ground, with his poll the highest point. His neck should arch forwards and upwards from his withers, just in front of the saddle.

Bend

Some parts of the horse's body bend more than others. The neck is the most flexible part and the hips the least flexible. His tail is very flexible. He can bend his spine from side to side, and up and down – so there is lateral and vertical movement in the saddle area, where the rider sits.

3.3 Turning together; both horse and rider looking forwards around the turn.

Over the centuries it was worked out that the most comfortable and effective place to sit on a horse is where we sit today. In the correct riding position, the rider's legs touch the horse on the most sensitive area on his sides, either side of the ribcage, behind the shoulders and elbows, where there are a lot of nerve endings. Watch your horse as a fly lands in this area and see how much he twitches to get rid of the fly!

This area behind the shoulders is where we say the horse bends from. In actual fact, it is not so much that the horse bends here, but he is able to swing his whole ribcage to the outside as he turns, rather like a barrel rolling. (Photo 3.3) His ribs move out of the way as he bends his lumbar area, placing his hind legs forwards under his body as he turns.

In order to bring his hind legs under his body to take weight behind as he turns, he needs to tuck his pelvis under and his spine has to lift to allow this to happen. To lift his spine, the horse needs to tighten his abdominal muscles. These run along the underside of his belly; you can see a muscle line here if your horse is working properly. If he is *not* working properly with his hind legs engaged, or underneath his back end, he will most likely look as though he has a beer belly and his hind legs will be out behind!

If your horse is working in balance and in a correct outline, therefore, he should turn easily.

How flexion and bend work together

To turn the horse, you must first prepare him for the turn. In essence, you need to point him in the direction in which you want him to go. This is known as positioning the horse and is the slightest flexion and bend that you are able to achieve. Your body positions the horse with this very slight flexion and bend as an indication of what is coming next before you actually perform the turn, circle or lateral movement. (Photo 3.4)

When riding a turn of any description, the flexion and bend must increase. A turn is about six strides on a curved line. Before a turn to the left, for example, the horse must be positioned left for a few strides and then the flexion must be increased so that his ears are on the curved line you wish to ride. His body must bend enough so he is evenly bent from nose ears to tail as he turns. (Photo 3.5)

Below left
3.4 The horse is in position right in preparation for a circle to the right.

Below right
3.5 The horse should bend from nose to tail as he turns.

To ride a circle, the horse must be flexed and bent consistently around the circle. For every stride he takes around the circle the horse must have the same flexion and bend, otherwise it is not a circle! Once the circle has been completed, the horse must be straightened so that he is merely positioned as opposed to bent and finally he should be straightened completely before being preparing for the next movement.

Positioning in preparation for a correct canter lead

Positioning the horse also applies to riding the canter. You need to position the horse to the left to get a transition to left-lead canter, and to the right for right-lead canter. (Photo 3.6)

When riding counter-canter, you must maintain the horse's position for the canter lead you are in.

With a flying change, you need to change both your and your horse's position, from left to right, or vice versa, at exactly the right moment when the horse is in the air, i.e. at the moment of suspension, to achieve a change of leg without losing the canter quality.

If you are riding tempi changes, keep the horse's head straight. There is not the time to flex his head at each change. This just looks very messy, and all that wiggling around will surely give the horse a headache! It is important for the rider

3.6 The horse is flexed at the poll and bent in the ribs in this left-lead canter.

to sit as still as possible, just changing their lower body position to indicate the change of lead to the horse; there is no need to throw your upper body all over the place, hurling the horse one way and then the other. Unfortunately this is seen all too often!

Circles and Turns

Inside and outside aids and their effect on circles and turns

The expression 'inside and outside aids' refers to the signals given to the horse when he is on a circle or turn, or positioned to the right or left. The inside of the bend is the direction the horse is flexed and/or bent towards. If he is flexed or bent to the left, his left side is the inside and if he is flexed or bent to the right, the right side is his inside.

A good illustration of this is if you place a banana on a table (no, I'm not joking!) curving to the left, its left side would be the inside, and the right side would be the outside of the bend if it were a horse! If it is placed so that it curves to the right, the right side is the inside, and the left side is the outside. I use the expression 'left banana' or 'right banana' frequently when teaching riders lateral work – a banana is a banana in most languages!

Your inside aids are on the inside of the bend of the horse, and the outside ones on the outside of the bend of the horse. (Photos 3.7a and b)

When riding in an arena some instructors will refer to the outside aids being on the side nearest the fence, and the inside aids on the side away from the fence. So what happens when you are in open country and want to ride a circle? If you bear in mind that 'inside' and 'outside' is simply the inside or outside of the bend of the horse, you will be able to ride and circle or turn accurately, even in the middle of a desert. (Just think of a banana lying on the desert sands!)

The positioning aids

To position your horse to the right or left, in preparation for a turn, circle or lateral movement, you need to position your body to the right or left. Start by making sure you are sitting tall and straight in the saddle, with your weight evenly on both seat bones. Your shoulders should be level and your hands parallel. Look straight ahead between the horse's ears. (Photos 3.8a and b)

I have described left positioning to explain the positioning aids and so for right positioning just reverse the aids.

Opposite, above
3.7a and b Turning with the horse. a) The outside aids. The outside leg is back just far enough to ask the horse to turn. The outside rein allows the horse to turn his neck and shoulders; it supports the turn without restricting it. b) The inside aids. The inside leg is by the girth to support the horse and asks for bend in the ribs. It also asks the inside hind leg to step forwards.

Opposite, below
3.8a and b Sitting straight: a) front view – looking forwards between the horse's ears; b) rear view – with the weight equal on both seat bones.

To ride in left position, turn your hips and upper body very slightly to the left. As you do this, keep your elbows by your sides and your hands in front of your body, so that they move slightly to the left with your body. Your hands must remain one each side of the horse's withers – the outside hand must not cross over the horse's neck – and they must remain parallel; remember the feeling of holding a small tea tray. Turn your head as well, keeping your chin in line with your chest. Lining it up with the zipper or buttons on the front of your jacket may help! (Photos 3.9a and b)

As you turn your body to the left, stretch your left leg down into the stirrup. Make sure your stirrup leather is perpendicular, with your weight on your toes, with a lowered heel. The leg must not be shoved forwards with your heel rammed down. This is now the inside leg. Its function is to ask the horse to bend by pressing your whole leg against the horse's side, and to step under with his inside hind leg with your calf (lower leg). It is also used to support the horse, to prevent him from cutting the turns or falling in, i.e. leaning to the inside and losing the correct inside bend.

Your right leg is now the outside leg. Press this stirrup down and back with, again, your weight on your toes with a lowered heel. Bring your whole leg back from the hip, do not bend your leg from the knee and raise the heel, as many riders do. The function of the outside leg is to ask the horse to turn initially. The lower leg activates the outside hind leg, for instance when asking for a canter strike-off, and pressure from your thigh (upper leg) controls the outside shoulder and

3.9a and b a) Positioning the horse to the left. b) Positioning the horse to the right.

prevents the horse from drifting wide when turning, or falling out, i.e. the horse is incorrectly bent to the inside and his outside shoulder leads the movement off course. (Photos 3.10a and b)

Keep your weight level on both seat bones. You do not need to sit to the inside, or put your inside hip forwards as is commonly taught. Simply turn your hips and keep your weight even on both sides of the saddle. If you do this, you will keep the horse balanced on both hind legs as he turns.

Keep your ribs lifted and in line with your hips. Your upper body should turn as one unit, including your head. If you collapse at the waist your horse will not turn but lean and go around the turn on 'two wheels' and not in 'four-wheel drive'! If you turn from the waist instead of your hips, your horse will not turn. Many riders turn their head and pull on the inside rein, but forget about the other aids, so the horse does not understand. He will turn his neck, but not bend; his haunches will fall to the outside as there is no control from the outside aids. The inside and outside aids are, therefore, just as important as each other and must be used in coordination.

Some horses bend more easily to the left, and some to the right. Horses are left-hinded or right-hinded, being stronger on one hind leg than the other, in the same way as we are left- or right-handed. Your aids may have to adapt to help the horse to flex and bend equally in both directions. This is what riding is all about, helping your horse to improve and become more athletic. For example, if your horse finds it more difficult to bend to the left, your aids may initially need to be firmer than when turning to the right.

3.10a and b a) The inside leg position by the girth. b) The outside leg position behind the girth.

Your job as a rider is to use various school exercises to help the horse to become more evenly balanced on both hind legs. If he leans on your inside rein when turning, he is showing you that he needs more support on that side, so your inside leg aids must be as firm as the rein aid to balance things out. Use frequent half-halts to rebalance the horse, making sure your inside and outside aids match in strength on both sides of the horse. A test of a good turn is to be able to soften the reins and keep turning!

The turning aids: how to ride a turn and a circle

To turn left, you need to position the horse to the left a few strides before the point you wish to turn at. This gives the horse some idea of what is coming next and avoids a last-minute panic. Indecision on your part will confuse your horse and you may not go where you want to. This is common in a dressage test when making a grand entrance down the centre line only to forget which way to turn at C as you approach the beady eye of the judge for the first time. (I know; I have done it myself many times!)

The arc of a right-angled turn should correspond to a quarter of a 10m circle. If your horse is supple and balanced, and at an advanced level in his training, you can ride turns more sharply, like a quarter of a smaller circle, or volte, of 6–8m in diameter.

A guide to riding accurate turns as a quarter of a 10m circle is to count six steps on a curved line: three on the way in to the turn, and three on the way out of it. At the halfway point, you should be at the apex or deepest part of the turn.

When you reach the starting point of the turn, use your outside leg to commence turning; use the upper and lower leg, plus knee pressure if your horse is reluctant to turn. Keeping your inside leg down by the girth, apply pressure with your lower leg to keep the horse stepping forwards with his inside hind leg to power through the turn, and your thigh to prevent him from falling in. At the same time, turn your body more: your head, chest, stomach, hips and hands should all line up with the arc of the turn. Your hands maintain a steady contact with both sides of the bit. Your outside hand eases forwards slightly to allow the horse to bend on the outside. The inside rein keeps the horse's nose on the arc of the turn – maintaining flexion. So in effect, to ride a turn, you use both legs, both hands and all of your body!

A 10m circle is four turns joined together. After each quarter of the circle, check that your body position is correct, you should have no problem in riding an accurate circle every time! Look forwards between the horse's ears as you ride the circle. Your chin should line up with your chest – try not to make the mistake of turning your head too much. Many riders look too far ahead around the circle, turning their heads to the side, and forget to turn their shoulders.

Give your leg aids in the rhythm of the horse's gait. This keeps the horse relaxed and if he is relaxed, he will swing through his back and work happily into a steady contact. Try to maintain rhythm, flexion and bend at every stride. This keeps everything ticking along nicely and avoids having to take emergency action should things go wrong. You may find that your horse falls in on the first half of a circle, and drifts out on the second half. If this happens, use firmer inside aids on the first half of the circle, and firmer outside aids on the second half. If you use your check points after each quarter of the circle, you should be able to prevent this from happening.)

Your circle should start and finish at exactly the same point. Each quarter of the circle should have the same arc, like four segments of an orange. (Have you noticed the unintentional fruit-based theme in this section?) For a smaller circle, turn your body more and use your inside leg more. To make the circle bigger, turn your body less as a shallower bend is required from the horse.

Changing Direction

Once you have established positioning the horse and how to ride a turn and circle, you can progress to changing direction accurately and in balance to enhance every aspect of riding you undertake.

How to change direction in balance

Between each turn in either direction, it is very important to straighten the horse for at least one step. When you are schooling your horse, or learning how to change direction you will need to ride several straight steps between right and left turns. This gives you a chance to make sure every little thing is correct. It does pay to attend to the small details. A minor error with the first turn will turn into a greater one with each successive turn, unless you put things right as you go. Prepare well for each change of direction and you will not go wrong, and your horse will remain in balance. If the preparation is *not* done, however, your horse will become less supple, he will lean on the reins for support if you are not using your body and legs correctly, and you will end up hauling him around the dressage arena/show-jumping course etc, or instead of enjoying a gentle hack out on a Sunday morning you may be heading for a collision with a tree in the woods!

As mentioned, we are all right- or left-handed and horses tend to be right- or left-hinded, and this will lead you to discover that you can turn more easily one way than the other, or that your horse is more supple in one direction than the other. To ride balanced turns in each direction in quick succession, however, your aids need to be mirror images of each other.

Earlier in the book we established that the simplest way to change from one direction to the other is to sit with your weight equally on both seat bones, which gives you control over both sides of the horse's back, and both hind legs, but many instructors will tell you to sit to the inside or to put your weight to the inside as you turn. This needs clarifying. Many riders interpret the use of the weight in this way as rather like riding a motorbike. They lean to one side and then the other, which makes the horse do the same thing. Leaning over also tempts the rider to turn the inside knee out, bringing the inside thigh and knee away from the horse.

If you sit with your weight on your inside seat bone, you need to make sure that you only have slightly more weight on this one than the outside seat bone; you do not put all your weight on the inside seat bone and none on the other. To be honest, the degree of weight to the inside needed to turn or change direction is minimal – it is much simpler to put a bit more pressure on the inside stirrup than the outside.

When you put pressure on the inside stirrup, just press the ball of your foot into the stirrup, and soften your ankle. This lengthens your inside leg and deters you from raising the knee in an effort to put more lower leg on. This weight into the stirrup encourages the horse to turn with you but it is also important to keep your legs against the horse's sides to help him to balance.

Your inside calf also has the function of asking the horse to keep moving and to step under his body with his inside hind leg. Your outside calf gives the initial aid to ask your horse to turn. Ask the horse to turn with your outside leg further back than the inside one. This positioning of your legs happens automatically as you turn your hips.

Use your outside calf to ask him to turn his back end, the haunches, and your outside knee and thigh to ask him to turn his forehand, i.e. the front end, or everything in front of the saddle from the shoulders to his ears. Turn your hips and shoulders at the same time, so the whole of your body turns with the whole of the horse's body.

As your body turns, your hands will take the bit with them, effectively turning the horse's head slightly at the poll, showing the horse the direction he is going in (flexion) and keeping his nose on the line you are riding.

After the initial turn, straighten your horse for a few steps, during which ride a half-halt (or more than one if necessary) to ensure your horse is in balance and taking weight behind. If he is not balanced, he will not bend properly in his body, and not have an even contact in both reins.

With an even contact, your horse should feel the same amount of pressure on both sides of his mouth and 'pressure' does not mean being heavy handed. Aim for the lightest feeling on the reins to keep the bit lying lightly against the horse's gums. If you can feel his jawbone, your contact is far too strong!

You should have the reins just tight enough to keep them straight, without them hanging in loops. Reins that are slack smack the bit around in the horse's mouth, which is not a pleasant experience for the horse. This often happens with riders who try to keep their hands still, rather than keeping the bit still in the horse's mouth – two very different scenarios. Trying to keep the hands still causes tension in the rider's arm joints: the shoulders, elbows and wrists. If you aim to keep the bit steady in the horse's mouth, you need flexible arm joints to act as shock absorbers; this is very important when changing direction.

The sequence for changing direction

Position your horse to the left and turn left by turning your body to the left and with the inside leg down into the stirrup, and your outside leg back, ease the outside (right) rein to allow the horse to turn. Keep your inside (left) rein still, maintaining the contact with the bit on both sides. Your hands will remain parallel with the horse's withers, either side of the pommel of the saddle. When turning, make sure you look between the horse's ears at all times.

Straighten him for a few steps with your hands, shoulders, hips, knees and feet parallel and check that you still have a steady contact with both sides of the bit.

Once you have straightened your horse, put him into right position, and ride a turn to the right. As you position the horse for a turn to the right, to change direction, ease your new outside (left) rein forwards to allow the horse to turn. When changing direction, make sure you straighten your head and shoulders at the same time, so you are looking straight between the horse's ears as you ride a straight step before repositioning him.

Rider Posture and its Influence on the Aids to Turn

When riding turns, circles and changes of direction, it is important that both horse and rider turn together. So often you see a rider hanging off the side of the horse, holding the inside rein down by the top of their boot; or leaning back with the inside foot rammed down onto the stirrup and hauling like mad on the inside rein. This has absolutely no effect whatsoever except to panic the horse who invariably tanks off in the opposite direction intended by the hapless rider!

Using just your arms and legs to guide the horse around invariably does not work. Unless you have strong core muscles and a focused mind, you will not be able to manoeuvre half a ton of horse around an arena – whether it be for dressage or jumping – or negotiate hazards when riding cross-country or hacking.

Engage your core muscles

To practise the body aids needed to turn your horse, stand in riding position on the ground, feet apart as though you were astride an invisible horse. In tai chi circles, this is actually known as the Horse Rider's Stance, so should you have the urge to take up martial arts, you should have an advantage over non-equestrians! (Photo 3.11)

Now engage your core muscles. If you need to remind yourself where your core muscles are and what it feels like to brace your back, familiarise yourself once more with the fence-rail exercise on page 56. You must use your body when bracing, not just your arms. If your arms are used alone, you will be pulling the horse. Bracing is in effect a half-halt; yes, half-halts crop up all the time – they are essential to keep the horse in balance!

So, once you have sorted out your core muscles, move away from the fence, and resume your riding position with your hands parallel.

Making the turn on the ground

To turn left, tighten your core muscles (I often describe this as though anticipating a punch in the stomach, though I do not recommend you ask someone to actually do this!) and turn your whole upper body, from the hips upwards, including your head, to your left. Your hands come with your body, remaining parallel with your hips and shoulders. (Photos 3.12a and b)

Below left
3.11 Standing in riding position with engaged core muscles for body control.

Below, centre and right
3.12a and b a) Turning to the left correctly with the upper body turning from the hips. Weight is placed on the inside foot. b) Turning to the right correctly. In both photos, as the hips turn, so the rider's inside and outside leg position is created. The hands are in front of the upper body, and the chin in line with the chest. The knees are bent and the ankles flexed.

As you turn, place a bit more weight on your inside foot (the left one) keeping your foot flat on the ground. Avoid twisting at the knee or ankle. A lot of people find it difficult to keep their hips central when doing this, and tend to push their hips to the outside (to the right when the turn is to the left), straightening their inside (left) knee in the process. Both knees should remain bent at the same angle.

The outside (right) leg presses down and back into the ground to stabilise your balance. If you put all your weight on your inside (left) foot, your outside leg would weaken and flail about in mid air. Yes, I have seen this frequently on horseback: the rider leans dramatically to the inside, and raises her outside heel, booting the horse to try to make him turn, accompanied by the aforementioned hand by the boot inside-rein position!

If you make this turning aid correctly when mounted, your horse will turn with you. Your inside leg supports your body weight as you turn and also supports the inside of the horse as he turns. It maintains the bend in his ribs by preventing them from bulging to the inside. You want your inside leg to press the horse's ribcage to the outside, creating the bend in his body. Imagine you have his ribcage between your legs, and are turning him with you.

Repeat this exercise to the right. You may find you turn more easily one way than the other, so practise until you can turn equally in both directions! (Photos 3.13a and b)

3.13a and b a) Preparing to circle to the left with the horse in left position. b) The rider uses the outside leg to commence the circle, turning the hips and shoulders together.

a

b

3.14 Widening the hands, keeping the elbows by the sides of the upper body, is very useful for controlling the horse's shoulders when turning. The rider's legs must be on the horse's sides for this to work.

Your knees and hips should turn with the horse and so avoid turning from the waist because if you do, your knees and hips will remain straight, and your horse will carry on regardless in a straight line. Your ankles should remain softly flexed at all times. Tightening the ankles will invariably affect your balance, and your knee and hip flexion will also be affected. Stiffening your legs creates tension, and your horse will not understand your leg aids to turn.

As you turn your upper body, keep your hands parallel and turn them as well. They should remain the same width apart, and your elbows should stay by your sides. It is all too easy to stick your inside elbow out and to bring your inside hand to the inside to 'lead' the horse around. If your horse does not grasp that you wish to turn and you need a back-up rein aid, open, i.e. widen, both hands into a big-tea-tray position, or as though you were opening the pages of a broadsheet newspaper. (Photo 3.14)

To make sure your hand position is correct when you turn, you could ask a willing friend to help you with an exercise. It may well help her with her own riding skills in the process, so she may thank you!

Stand facing each other in riding position. Hold a rope between you. You need to hold what would be the rein end of the rope, while your friend acts the part of the horse with both her hands closed around the middle of the rope, substituting for the horse's mouth. The rope she's holding will be the bit. Turn your body to the left from the hips bringing your horse with you. If you do it properly, your horse will happily follow your lead as you turn the bit with both reins, hands and arms. If you turn from your waist, however, nothing will happen. Your horse will not feel the guiding effect of the turn coming from your whole body. It is a very interesting exercise to try; you may feel a bit silly, but it really does give you the idea of how your horse will respond to your turning aids, or not as the case may be! Repeat the exercise to the right with mirror-image aids. (Photo 3.15)

It is very important to find your own weaknesses on the ground. If it goes wrong it is usually the rider that is wrong – not the horse.

COMMON PROBLEMS

- **Lack of flexion.** Instead of using both hands to maintain the contact when asking for flexion with the whole body position, many riders just increase the pressure on the inside rein. This can cause nose tipping rather than flexion (Photo 3.16). The horse's ears will no longer be level, so this will unbalance the turn.

- **Too much neck bend.** It is a very common sight to see riders pulling like mad on the inside rein in their attempts to turn their horses. The poor horses have

3.15 Practise turning a friend using a rope as the reins. Here, Lorraine is turning me, and I am following the direction her body is taking me in (to her right).

3.16 This photo shows the horse tipping his nose to the inside in canter.

their necks cranked around, often with their noses on the riders' inside knees. I think the theory must be: if you pull his head around far enough he will turn. This may be the case, but the horse will neither be balanced nor prepared for any particular movement and will turn simply to relieve himself of the discomfort he must surely be in rather than to work in accord with the rider. (Photos 3.17a and b, see overleaf)

The horse's neck is a very bendy part of the body, and it will twist a long way around before the horse feels the need to move in the direction his head is pointing. A stiff horse, on the other hand, who is unable to turn his neck very far, will take evasive action by swinging his haunches away from the direction the rider is trying to go in.

There is a standard stretching exercise you can try with your horse to see how bendy he is on the ground, namely: 'carrot stretches'. Stand your horse parallel, and close, to a wall of his stable. Hold a carrot, or any other titbit he favours, in your hand on his side by his belly. Encourage him to stretch his neck around to eat the titbit. Repeat in the other direction; you will need to turn him around so his other side is by the wall.

When schooling your horse, make sure his neck stays in line with his shoulders. He must bend from his ribcage, in the location of your inside leg, and flex at the poll in the direction he is going. As a guide, your horse's nose should not be further to the inside of the bend than the point of his inside shoulder. (Photo 3.18, see overleaf)

Above, left and centre
3.17a and b a) Too much neck bend to the rider's right, and (b) too much neck bend to the rider's left.

Above, right
3.18 Correct neck bend when turning – the horse's nose should be no further to the side than the point of the inside shoulder.

Remember, if you are trying to turn by pulling on the inside rein, this a sure sign that you are not turning your body.

- **Changing speed around turns and circles; going either too fast or too slow.** Not maintaining a regular rhythm and tempo when riding different school moves, such as turns, circles and serpentines is also a common problem.

Often, the rider will go fast along straight lines, only to slow down when turning. Going too fast puts more weight on the horse's forehand and makes it difficult for him to turn. Consequently the rider overcompensates and slows down too much for the turn. He may also sound heavy-footed as he pounds along! Because the turn is undoubtedly unbalanced and inaccurate, the horse speeds up after the turn. The rider slows right down for the next turn, and so the vicious circle continues.

Going too fast when turning results in a lack of suppleness. The horse becomes tense because he is being pushed out of his natural rhythm. Because he is tense, he becomes tight in his body, and is unable to bend. Consequently, his haunches swing out, so the horse goes around the turns on 'two wheels' instead of in 'four-wheel drive'. His weight is thrown to the inside shoulder to compensate for the lack of weight he is able to take on his hind legs i.e. he is unable to take weight behind. The rider is usually in hyper-drive in this situation; they need to take their foot off the gas pedal! (Photo 3.19)

Turning too slowly results in lack of traction and power from the haunches. The horse's strides shorten as a consequence, and the activity is lost in the leg joints, resulting in the horse dragging his feet. The most obvious sign of this is that he kicks up the ground surface with each step. (If there is no dust, your

Far left
3.19 If you go too fast, your horse will lose suppleness and not be able to bend as he turns and will drift out through his outside shoulder.

Left
3.20 Leaning in on a circle causes the horse to 'motorbike'.

horse is moving well!) He may well hollow his back and lose the connection to the bit. He will no longer be in a correct rounded outline and appear to sag in the middle!

The slowing down is often accompanied by a lack of balance, with the horse's hind legs trailing out behind. He may also lose direction and drift out or fall in when turning. In this situation, the rider is being too wishy-washy with their aids and position!

- **Cutting turns.** Riders often lean in when turning their horses, thinking they are on a bicycle or motorbike (Photo 3.20, see above). They usually lean forwards also and give the outside rein away (Photo 3.21, see overleaf). They stick their inside knee out, bringing the inside thigh away from the saddle, which then no longer supports the horse in the turn. This rider position often occurs when the rider is using too much inside rein to turn. They may twist from the waist rather than turn at the hips. The rider may lean in in an effort to 'sit on the inside seat bone'. The horse will tend to swing his haunches out, as he is unable to step forwards with his inside hind leg due to the rider being in the way and blocking his back on the inside. Simply keeping the weight on both seat bones will rectify this. The rider then has to turn their hips and shoulders correctly.

Right
3.21 On the ground: leaning forwards and giving the outside rein away and twisting at the waist to the left.

Far right
3.22 On the ground: leaning in rather than turning. The rider's weight is on the outside foot, she is leaning in and 'driving the bus', and the hands are not parallel.

- **Falling out around turns.** The rider's weight is not central on the horse's back. You must sit on both seat bones to control both hind legs. If the weight is to the outside you may be leaning back and sitting to the outside, or leaning out. In either case, the weight will be in the way of the outside hind leg stepping forwards under the horse's body. It is important to control the outside of the horse with the outside rein and leg, keeping the hands parallel. (Photo 3.22)

  The horse may place this hind foot across to the inside to counter balance the rider's weight. This affects the horse's straightness, i.e. prevents the hind feet following in the tracks of the forefeet (think of it as being in four-wheel drive, or the horse going on two parallel tracks, like railway lines, as he turns). The horse may well bend the wrong way, to the outside, in his efforts to compensate for the unbalanced rider on board! (Photo 3.23)

- **Placing the inside leg too far back.** Sometimes riders can have a very good inside leg position when turning, but they can tend to bring the lower leg too far back to give an aid (Photo 3.24). They may also draw the leg up instead of keeping their weight down in the stirrup. The knack is to keep the leg down and in the same place on the horse's side when applying pressure with the calf, knee and thigh. The leg pressure should be forwards rather than backwards. A backwards leg aid, even if the lower leg has not moved out of place, will tend to push the horse's haunches out. A forwards leg aid presses against the horse's side in the direction of the rider's outside hand. This creates bend,

3.23 The horse's body is not on the circle line from nose to tail; his hind feet are not following the tracks of the front feet.

3.24 Here, the rider's inside leg is too far back in this canter.

asks the horse to go forwards and supports the horse all at the same time. How clever is that?!

• **Bending the outside leg back from the knee.** This a common mistake made by many riders. Just bringing the lower leg back and flapping it around is not a very effective outside leg aid! They should be drawing the outside thigh back, which is far more effective (this should happen anyway if the rider is turning their hips correctly) and the whole leg can then be used to turn the horse. The outside thigh and knee will help the forehand to turn, and the lower leg will prevent the haunches from swinging out.

Riding turning exercises

Turning exercises can be based on circles with a consistent bend; squares and rectangles, turns linking straight lines; figures of eight, changing direction from one circle to another; or serpentines, a series of loops alternating between bending right and left.

RIDDEN EXERCISES

All the following exercises should be ridden on both reins.

Turn Exercise 1

Riding squares Starting at X in walk, trot or canter, have your horse in left position and ride a 20m square to the left. Make sure the turns are all the same size; aim for a quarter of a 10m circle for each one. As you return to the centre point of the school, at X, straighten for a step or two, and change your position, so that your horse is positioned to the right. Ride a square to the right. (Diagram 9)

Turn Exercise 2

Spiralling in and out on a circle Ride a 20m circle around X. Gradually spiral in, until your circle is about 10m in diameter. Spiral out again. As you spiral in, increase bend and flexion. As you spiral out, reduce bend and flexion. (Diagram 10)

Turn Exercise 3

Riding a serpentine Ride a three-loop serpentine starting at A; as you reach the quarter line 5m in from the track, ride the first loop to the left (about 13m in diameter, equivalent to one third of the school). Between the quarter lines (shown as grey dashed lines on Diagram 11, see overleaf) ride straight. As you reach the second quarter line, commence a second loop, this time to the right, the same

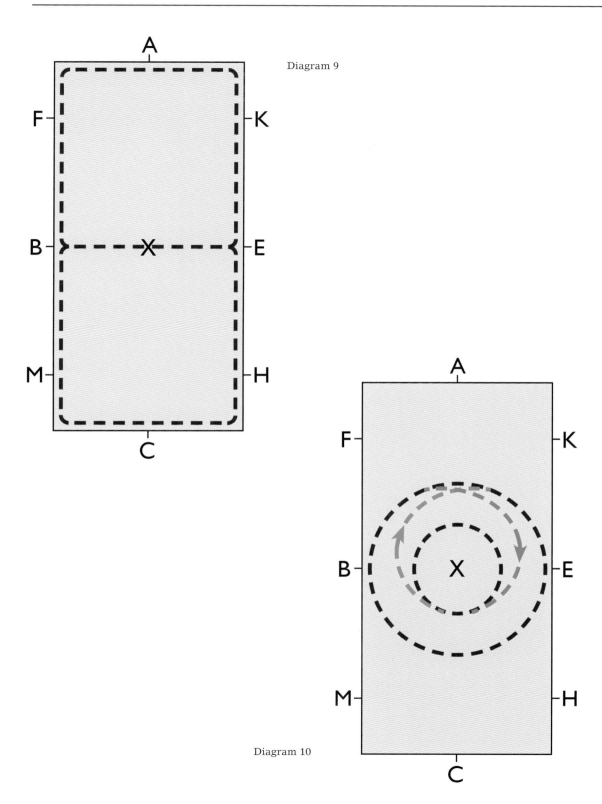

Diagram 9

Diagram 10

Diagram 11

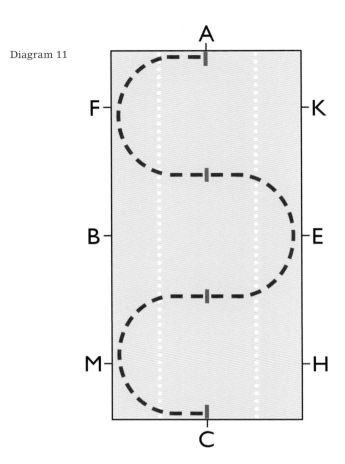

diameter as the first loop. Ride straight across between the quarter lines. Ride the third loop to the left, finishing the serpentine at C. Make sure the loops are the same size and shape. Ride the serpentine on the other rein, starting from C and making the first loop to the right.

You could progress to serpentines of four loops, with each loop 10m in diameter.

Serpentines can be ridden in walk, trot or canter. In canter, you could ride a change of lead between the quarter lines, either through trot or walk.

Turn Exercise 4

Riding a figure of eight in canter and counter-canter Starting at X, position your horse to the left and ride a 20m circle to the left. Remember to ride a minimum of one step straight as you change direction on returning to X. Position your horse to the right, and ride a 20m circle to the right. Gradually reduce the size of the figure of eight to 10m circles in either direction.

This can be ridden in walk, trot or canter. If you are riding it in canter, you can either change the lead through trot or walk at X, or halt over X before striking off again on the opposite lead. You could also ride this exercise without changing the canter lead at X. Thus you will ride one circle in true canter, and the other in counter-canter. (Diagram 12)

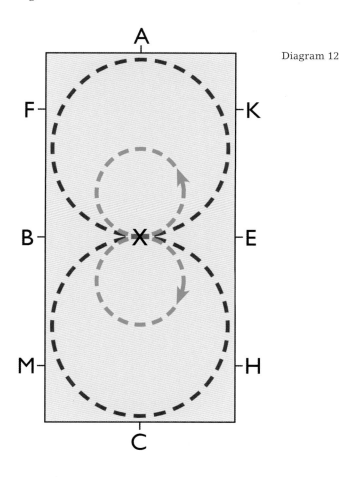

Diagram 12

Conclusion

In any sport, it is essential to learn key skills, without which you will not progress. The golfer will spend hours at the driving range perfecting his swing. The tennis player will practise his different strokes day in, day out. Riding is no different. There is no magic formula for creating a better partnership with your horse; only patient schooling. Being able to stop, go and turn is fundamental to making progress with your horse in any sphere. I hope this book will help you on your way to success. Happy riding!

Index